A Sensitive, Passionate Man

Barbara Mahoney

DAVID McKAY COMPANY, INC.
NEW YORK

A SENSITIVE, PASSIONATE MAN

Permission to quote material from:

New Primer on Alcoholism by Marty Mann has been granted by the courtesy of Holt, Rinehart and Winston, Inc.

The selection from *Personae* by Ezra Pound, copyright 1926 by Ezra Pound, has been reprinted by permission of New Directions Publishing Corporation.

LIBRARY OF CONGRESS CATALOG CARD NUMBER: 73–91118
ISBN: 0–679–50443–5
MANUFACTURED IN THE UNITED STATES OF AMERICA
Designed by E. O'Connor

1789671

For our sons

Preface

When I was seven I used to play with the boy next door, an only child, and whenever I went to his house, a dark, gloomy place, the maid invariably cautioned us to be quiet, for the boy's mother was always lying in bed, resting. I was told that she had TB.

Sometimes, when she was strong enough, she would come over to visit my mother, and even if it was eleven o'clock in the morning, she'd pull a small silver flask out of her purse and say in her soft Southern voice, "Here, Betty, I brought us a little treat. Let's have a highball."

I liked her. Although she had gotten fat around the middle, she had a pretty face and a very sweet manner; and I liked the way she smelled, a kind of mixture of Scotch and soda and perfume.

She died several years later. I overheard my mother whisper that it was cirrhosis, and when I asked what that was, it turned out to be a disease of the liver and not of the lungs.

When my husband died, an obituary writer called from *The New York Times* to check out the facts. "It says your husband died after a long illness. . . . It was cancer, wasn't it?"

"No," I answered, "it was cirrhosis."

"Oh," he said thoughtfully. "Well then, we'll just say 'after a long illness.' "

It wasn't quite acceptable—or nice or proper—to die of cirrhosis thirty years ago, and it still isn't today. Cirrhosis means that one probably died of drink, that one therefore was a drunk, or, in pathological terms, an alcoholic, for alcoholism is said to be a disease.

However, there was no mention of the disease of alcoholism in the autopsy report. After examining my deceased husband's shriveled liver, the doctor concluded in "our final findings" that he had died of "very advanced cirrhosis of the liver." In polite, clinical terms he explained exactly what had happened:

> In this disease, scar tissue replaces large amounts of the functioning cells of the liver. The liver is an important organ in detoxifying many substances that come from the intestine, in processing various food materials into forms that are useful for the body, and in excreting breakdown products of red blood cells. All of these functions were severely impaired, and, in addition, the scar tissue greatly interfered with the flow of blood through the liver by obstructing veins.

Anatomy One-A. But then, less didactically, almost wistfully:

> The amount of liver tissue found in our examination was extremely small and incompatible with life.

And, by way of polishing off the report, the following fusty rationale:

The cause of this disease in the liver is usually thought to be nutritional or the result of interference with liver-cell metabolism by alcohol, or the combination of both.

In my husband's case I believe the cause of cirrhosis was entirely due to alcohol rather than to poor nutrition. Throughout the years of heavy drinking he was always aware of the sustaining powers of food, and when he was too sick or broke to eat anything else he kept going on potato salad or soup or milk, and to the end he was still trying to down the tasteless hospital food. Moreover, I believe that he actually died of the disease of alcoholism and that the cirrhosis was simply the final symptom of the sickness that caused him to drink himself to death.

And further, I'm convinced that the disease of alcoholism is far more "incompatible with life" than the cirrhosis. In addition to causing scar tissue to replace large amounts of the functioning cells of his liver, the disease destroyed his career and self-respect, decimated our marriage, and, though it is too soon to know the long-term effects, his long sickness, his alcoholism, is bound to have caused permanent scar tissue on the psyches of our four sons. As painful as it is to watch a father die, it is worse to witness the deterioration of his soul.

And yet, in one way, and in one way only, we were fortunate. At least my husband's illness didn't go on and on and he didn't end up on Skid Row or locked away for life in a mental institution. He died in a semiprivate room in a first-rate New York City hospital, attended by a first-rate Park Avenue internist—the very same doctor, in fact, whom I had called on exactly five years before my husband died, desperately looking for a way to help my alcoholic.

A Sensitive, Passionate Man

1

May 1965

It was the sleeping all day, almost more than anything else, that really got me. The sad, utter hopelessness, the giving up. Here was my warm, wonderful husband, holed up in the apartment, sleeping his precious life away. Standing in our silent living room, gazing numbly out of the ninth-floor windows across the city to the gleaming silver spire of the Chrysler Building, I wondered whether Rip Van Winkle had been an alcoholic.

Once there had never been enough time, time to get it all said, time for love, time for work and derring-do; and now there was nothing but time, long, endless, empty hours filling up our six rooms—one of his lucky finds seven years ago, the Upper East Side, rent-controlled, the right address at the right rent for an up-and-coming young lawyer, a way station en route to a co-op around the corner on Park. Or was it now the end of the line?

My Harvard Law School graduate, my Phi Beta Kappa, had set out on the road to the top, Wall Street, the Establishment, the green pastures of the legal trade, the golden mecca for the class of 1950, and somewhere along the line he had lost his way. At forty, Sean was lost, but we were still locked into the life, set up for it, the apartment in town, house in the country, children in private schools, locked in but shut out, blocked.

Shortly after eight that morning I had walked our four sons up Park Avenue to their school, smiling and nodding at other parents along the way but noticing especially the fathers; they looked so pulled together, so purposeful, striding along in their neatly pressed suits, Brooks Brothered for the day, armed for action with attaché cases and *The New York Times.* That's the way it was, the way he used to be, only somehow now he was stumbling around the apartment in his wrinkled white undershorts or sprawled across the bed.

I said goodbye to the boys, watched as they bounded inside the school, and then continued to stand by the door, trying to think of what to do next. It was too early for my usual hangouts: the Metropolitan Museum, only two blocks from home, a soothing place to wander; the Society Library on Seventy-ninth Street, a refuge of sedate reading rooms and musty stacks, the best escape hatch in town for twenty dollars' annual dues. And I was too tired for one of my long window-shopping walks down Madison to Fifty-seventh Street, topped off by a tour of Bloomingdale's.

Of course, there was always church. That was always open for the eight-o'clock Mass, and I had gone there often, sometimes two or three times a week, praying for one of those miracles I had read about in my literature on alcoholism, but this morning I was too depressed to believe in miracles. Eight in the morning was said to be a popular time to see a psychiatrist, but then I wasn't the one who needed treatment.

The sidewalk cleared of parents, nurses, and children, and I felt self-conscious still standing there, a displaced person, too alone; so there was nothing to do but take my tired and depressed self back to the apartment. I made a quick decision to walk via

Lexington Avenue. It was less pristine than Park, almost seedy, but more diverting, the street a jumble of buses, trucks, cabs, and cars, and the sidewalks crowded with people, all of whom appeared to have someplace to go or something to do. The vegetable-store man was putting out his vegetables, the newspaper man was making change, pedestrians were jockeying for position, trying to beat the light, to catch a bus, to flag a cab, to start the day. I envied them, one and all, and arrived at our corner all too soon.

I quietly let myself into the apartment, quietly did the breakfast dishes, quietly picked up the living room, quietly made the children's beds, first quietly and carefully closing our adjoining bedroom door so as not to awaken my sleeping husband. And then, when it was all done, there was nothing left to do, nothing but to stand at the window and quietly agonize: What in the name of God had gone wrong?

It was a sparkling spring morning, clear and sunny and warm at last. It was the first of May. ("Hurray, hurray," we used to say, "outdoor screwing begins today!") Our wedding anniversary was coming up on May 12—fourteen years of married love and, before that, five years of unmarried love, half my life in terms of time, but really all my life. The first part had been only the prelude, a long-short, capsulated, since-shoved-aside time of waiting for Sean to appear and pull the pieces together.

We met on a blind date during the Christmas holidays in 1946. I was twenty, biding my time as a model at Henri Bendel's, waiting to return to college in the spring, in the process of transferring from Berkeley to Bennington. I was ready to get back to the books, but I felt a bit rudderless, not quite sure where I was headed in life, and going back to college was, in a way, just a means of ducking out and starting over again. I had already given up trying to be an actress.

In my two years at the University of California I had rapidly worked myself up from bit parts to leads, and in June of 1946 I quit school to come to New York, where my sister Pat, a researcher on *Life*, was living, and to try my luck on Broadway. After three months of running around to casting offices, the only offer I had was a walk-on as a towel-draped masseuse in a Borscht-circuit production of *Up in Mabel's Room*. The producer hadn't even asked me to read, just grunted, like in an old Ruby Keeler movie, "Lemme see your legs." At Cal I had done *Electra* and *Candida*, and the thought of going out on the road in a risqué, even dirty, show like *Mabel's Room* was demeaning, but I steeled myself to taking the part and called my father in Washington to ask for the hundred dollars I needed to join Equity. He said no, that he didn't want me mixed up with those kinds of people in that kind of play, and I was tremendously relieved. It was a way of giving up and still keeping face with myself, these being the days when parents still made the big decisions. But I was also disappointed in myself.

I wished I could be more aggressive. *Mademoiselle* magazine was full of pictures of snappy, happy young women, ebullient with drive and determination, cutting wide swaths through the career world, while I was slouching around Bendel's, bored to death with my job, hiding out in the dressing room to read. For a while I'd run around on my lunch hour trying to get a more interesting job, on a magazine or in publishing, but I could never land one, and so during the fall I had decided to throw in the career towel and go back to college. Studying was definitely preferable to the frustrations of the career world as I had known it so far. I applied to Bennington, where my best friend, Gina, went, and was accepted with a scholarship for the 1947 spring semester. That was gratifying, but, still, my life lacked direction.

Once, before giving up as an actress, I had met Richard Aldrich, the producer and husband of my idol, Gertrude Lawrence. He was charming and gently told me I was a lovely girl, and instead of thinking about Broadway I should marry a nice man and have nice children. That was more or less the way I felt, too, only I could never quite convince myself that I was in love.

For the first several months in New York it had been great fun dancing and drinking in places I had always heard about, but now it had begun to seem rather pointless, and the notebook I kept read more like a bar card than a diary: "Three Scotches at the Monkey Bar, dinner and wine at Luchow's, on to the Pierre for stingers and dancing. Bill's a bore."

I wondered if I were too much of a loner, albeit a convivial one, even a party girl at times, but nonetheless a solitary. That's the way I often felt when I was growing up.

My parents had had an unhappy marriage, and by the time I graduated from high school I had gone to eight schools in the twelve years and had had as many addresses. My mother kept leaving my father, a government attorney in Washington, D.C., and off we'd go to Florida, living in a rented, furnished house or apartment, never poor but always short of cash. (It always rankled Mother that Daddy didn't make more money, but, having survived the Depression, he was content with mere security.) After a year or two we'd return to yet another rented house in another neighborhood in Washington while my parents tried to make another go of their marriage. This was in the Thirties, when divorce was still a slightly shady word, and I guess they thought that by sticking it out, even on an on-and-off basis, they were doing right by my sister and me. Finally, when I was seventeen, Mother went to Reno, and then she decided to live in San Francisco, which is how I ended up at Berkeley. Nothing was planned in our family; it just happened.

Though I never once doubted their love for me, it would have been kinder had they gone their separate ways sooner. When they were together the tension could be cut with a knife, and life was far more relaxed and pleasant when they were apart. But either way, I never felt I was part of an established way of life, a structure, and I envied my peers who were more securely placed, the ones who grew up in the same house with the same parents and went to the same neighborhood schools. They had an assurance that came from belonging, whereas I never felt I belonged anywhere, either physically or socially. I was a perpetual outsider.

In time I became used to the role and, to compensate, developed my own kind of assurance. I became adept at making new friends and adjusting to new schools, and once beyond the stresses and strains of childhood I counterbalanced the need to be sanctioned as one of the "ins" by deliberately turning my back on the pack. I gravitated toward those who did their own thing rather than the group-oriented (sorority life at Cal struck me as utterly jejune), and though I was lonely sometimes, I didn't mind being alone. I liked it. It was easier than trying to conform and also more interesting. It gave me a chance to sort out my own feelings, to get my own balance and make my own judgments. The negative side was that being a loner at twenty made it hard to see a pattern to life. I knew I really didn't want to be one of those dynamic, dedicated young career women in *Mademoiselle*. I wanted to love a man, not a job. That meant taking the other route, marriage. But from what I had seen of marriage, it was a risky road to hazard. So I felt a little lost. And then I met Sean and everything fell into place.

Gina introduced us. I was living with Pat in a tiny Village apartment, and Gina came down from Bennington to stay with us at the start of her Christmas vacation. As soon as she arrived we settled down to smoke and talk, and she told me that she had met a wonderful guy at Williams and that she had found the perfect man for me too. He was twenty-two, a senior, a veteran of three years in the Infantry, and a wheel in his fraternity. He had a Phi Beta Kappa key and a Purple Heart and planned to go to Harvard Law the following fall. Everyone thought he was brilliant and charming, the only drawback being that he was poor, and we could drink only beer on the double date she had arranged for the following night.

"My so-called dream man sounds like a superannuated Andy Hardy," I said, laughing, "but at least it will be a new experience."

I had never dated college boys. Pearl Harbor was bombed when I was fifteen, and by the time I was ready for college boys they were all in the service. There had been some ROTCs at Berkeley, but I bypassed them for ensigns and jg's and took no part in campus social life.

With Gina and her Williams beau, the four of us set off for Ed Winston's Tropical Bar and Grill on nearby Eighth Street. I had suggested Ed Winston's because it was a nicely sloppy, noisy spot, cheap but colorful. I figured that was what college boys would like; and on first impression there was no mistaking the fact that my blind date was a college boy, horn-rimmed glasses, black knit tie, tweed sports coat and all. And yet he didn't talk the way I thought college boys would talk. In fact, he didn't talk like anyone I had ever known. He ignored the raucous charm of Ed Winston's and with the first round of beers immediately plunged into an analysis of the ECA, of Truman and his give-'em-hell politics, of Sartre and his Existentialism, and of something called "the extrapolation of the finite perspective," whatever that was. He had an easy, quiet voice, and I found myself leaning forward to catch his words over the din. I wondered if he talked this way all the time or was just showing off.

During the war when I was dating all those sparkling blue-and-white ensigns and jg's, we were caught up in the eat-drink-and-be-merry syndrome, and we spent our time "partying"— dancing, drinking, necking, laughing, having a ball, forgetting the war was on. When the war ended, the party spirit continued in the first exhilarating rush back into civilian life, and a year later, by the time I came to New York in 1946, the transition from wartime to peacetime was complete. The men I dated in the city were in their late twenties or early thirties, and talk consisted largely of their current new office life, humorous high spots of their previous college or service life, and, in their inevitable future married life, whether to live in the suburbs or the city. Digressions were directed to the advantages of Brooks Brothers shirts (the new pink ones were always good for a little debate as to whether they were too flashy or too fairy for office wear), the latest gadgets at Hammacher's or Abercrombie's, the new car models, life-style decision-making being a matter of whether we should drink beer at P. J. Clarke's or go dancing at the Coq Rouge.

The really big question was whether to do it or not to do it. We talked a lot about sex. However, there was no final action, because even my most ardent beaux knew that only the really fast girls went all the way (except if you were engaged and months of prolonged necking and petting sessions had gotten out of control). But times were changing, and it was intriguing to discuss the pros and cons of free love. I was terribly curious (would it be like in *The Fountainhead*, an act of rage, a violation, or a close-your-eyes-and-think-of-England experience?), but the talking kept me pure. It made intercourse sound like an isolated act, a self-conscious, calculated experiment, so I resisted, though wondering what I was missing. But other than the fact of my virginity, there were no burning issues to ignite the conversational fires of my New York dates. Those had gone away with the war, submerged in the pleasant complacency of the peace. The social revolutions of the Sixties were still two decades away, and in 1946 the unexamined life was quite worth living as time stretched comfortably ahead in the progressive stages of material gain.

My college boy was different. He had an intensity, a kind of magnetic inner energy and restlessness to get to the point that made every second count. It showed in his darting, deep-set eyes; in the quick, chopping movement of his hand emphasizing a point; in the way he angled his head, his sharp, lean jaw thrust forward; even in the way he danced, holding me too closely, as if I might get away. (Surprisingly, he was an excellent dancer; somehow that didn't go with all the heady talk.) Though he was boyishly young-looking, I decided that he was attractive. I liked his warm, quick, one-sided grin that showed very even white teeth and the way he often threw back his head in laughter, a person who obviously got a big boot out of life. But he seemed much more interested in talking to his classmate than to me, and by midnight, bored with the beer and the free education, I decided I preferred older, less committed types who could afford Scotch.

It was after one o'clock when we finally left, and as we said good night at my door (Gina and her beau were downstairs necking) he asked me, almost as an afterthought, if I would like to go to the theater the following night. I said yes, mainly because I liked going to the theater; but the next day, parading around Bendel's in my finery, weary with a beer hangover, I regretted my decision.

However, the play was good. *Cyrano de Bergerac* with José Ferrer. Naturally, he had read it and I had not, but we were on more common ground, and the conversation was now two-sided. But immediately afterward we went to a bar to meet one of Sean's economics professors, and once again an in-depth analysis of the current international scene ensued. Because I had always been too much of a dreamer to know or care about politics, there was nothing for me to do but listen. I was impressed by his rapport with the professor, none of this me-student, you-teacher business I had known at Cal, but I was tired of being out of it and tired from the night before, and after several whispered pleas to leave, I stood up and announced I was going home.

The economics lecture continued all the way downtown in the cab. I only half listened, wondering if he ever ran down, and as it was already past midnight, I glumly programmed my next working day's exhaustion. He interrupted himself to tell the driver to stop. "Let's have a nightcap," he said, leaning across me to open the door. We were in front of a little bar on Tenth Street and, robotlike, I followed him inside.

It was a small place, a few steps down from the sidewalk, mostly long mahogany bar, a few tables, a mellow, soft place with an unobtrusive bartender and no piped-in music. I no longer know if such places still exist, but for many years thereafter we found them wherever we went, cozy retreats where we could sit and have a drink and talk away the hours. We used to wonder how other couples could find life so dreary as to sit together in silence, gazing beyond each other in a bind of mutual boredom.

He ordered brandies, and then the lecture stopped and we two started to talk. I had been waiting all my life for this to happen.

It wasn't that Sean knew more than anyone I had ever met but that he cared more, and cared with such spontaneous, dynamic warmth that each moment came alive, unique and glowing and totally personal. There was no bombast in his speech, no clichés; life itself was too absurd to need hyperbole. And also too precious.

Even his war stories were different, without the usual recourse to SNAFU humor or documentary monologues and table-cloth map-making that made the holocaust sound as if it had all taken place in the newsreels and comic strips. He was proud of his three years as a foot soldier and spoke of the war with fascination, a mix of fear, camaraderie, loneliness, exhilaration, loyalty, and sorrow, laced together with cold mud and kind civilians and the novelty and excitement of finding himself in Europe. Though I pressed him, he wouldn't talk about actual fighting except to say that he always carried something to read and, when he was shot, read *Time* cover to cover while he waited in a foxhole for the medics. He said he knew all along that he would survive but that it was sheer good luck when so many others hadn't. "Life can be a bitch," he explained, grinning, "and it's four o'clock in the morning." I liked his bravura.

When we went outside it was snowing, big, fat, white polka dots sifting softly across the dim, silent street. He was taking the noon train home to Massachusetts for Christmas, and there were still too many things that had to be said, so we strolled as slowly as possible back to my apartment, stopping under every awning to kiss. But, inevitably, we covered the two short blocks and were there.

"Come back to the Biltmore with me," he whispered as we huddled against the door. For the first time in my life, to do it or not to do it was no longer the question. I really wanted to go with him, and the word "no" wouldn't come. I smiled and shook my head, constrained by only the most tenuous of threads that said nice girls don't.

He wrote, asking me up to Williams, but I couldn't get away from work on Saturdays for the weekend. In February he sent me a valentine that said *"Vas is los?* You and I were once so close?" and asked me to winter house parties, but I'd had other plans, and we didn't meet again until I arrived on the Bennington campus early in March. The all-female student body was returning after a long winter work period away from school, and on the first night back Sean drove over with a carload of Williams students, monks escaping the monastery fifteen miles away on icy Route 7 for a look-see at the newly arrived inmates of the nunnery. We all sat in the dorm living room drinking beer. Sean appeared to be very much in tune with the rah-rah scene, but I felt disoriented. My erstwhile lover seemed younger than I remembered, and I missed the intimacy and immediacy of our date in New York.

Bennington social life, I discovered, was swamped in hearty conviviality, with mass congeniality enforced by rules and regulations (no men in the rooms after 6:00 P.M., no men on campus after 10:00 P.M.) and buttressed by the zero-degree weather that meant that at night everyone had to be inside someplace along with everybody else, be it the dorm or the State Line Bar. Sean and I had several dates, always enmeshed in a group, and I continued to feel estranged, as if I only half knew him. But the conviviality burst into full bloom when I went to my first Saturday-night cocktail party at his fraternity house.

The spacious entrance hall and living room were jam-packed with page-boyed girls, resplendent in their best wool dresses and high heels, and sports-jacketed men, all carefully groomed and brushed for the roistering, boisterous, laughing, chattering get-together. Everyone was exuberantly downing either the Purple

Passion punch or the safer martinis, the point being to get as fried as possible as fast as possible to assure ample bonhomie to carry through the formal fraternity dinner, preceded by a traditional little blessings-on-this-house by one of the less tipsy brothers. I poured down the martinis, trying to be one of the crowd, but the drinks make me feel even more of a spectator.

After the fruit cocktail, roast beef, and ice cream, a period of sedateness ensued, with the somewhat sobered-up participants gathering for coffee and quiet conversation in the living room, accompanied by soft meanderings on the piano. Gradually the room emptied as couples drifted upstairs. I wondered if the time had come when we were actually going to be alone. Sure enough, Sean, who had been engrossed in conversation with two other students, turned and casually asked if I would like to have a drink in his rooms.

Curled up on the couch in his living room, I watched, our two minds working as one, as he poured a large dash of bourbon into my beer. When the love-potion boilermaker was gone, I held out my glass for another, intent on getting even more tight, sweeping away forever the last remaining threads of inhibitions and moral strictures. And then we were in bed and he was making love to me.

On the way back to Bennington at 4:00 A.M. we stopped for coffee at an all-night diner. I had gone to sleep and now felt sober, very alive and wonderfully close to him. My memories of love-making were totally dim. But that didn't matter. I no longer just half knew him. I had escaped my virginity, he was now my lover, and we could go onward from there.

We were, as he said, as happy as clams at high tide.

The Productive Life

1947–1954

As the apple-blossom-scented spring came to Vermont, we walked and talked and made love in sunny mountain meadows and under the stars in nearby Bennington fields, touching, talking, feeling, sharing a warmth I had never known existed. Sean was an endearing lover, neither shy nor self-conscious nor selfish, a sensitive, passionate man, and physical closeness was as natural and necessary to our relationship as talk, and there couldn't have been one without the other.

In June he graduated, *cum laude*, and in the fall of 1947 went off to Harvard Law School. That ended the easy proximity between Williamstown and Bennington, but it didn't end our affair. In those long-gone pre-pill days, sleeping together—as it was called—wasn't the usual Ivy League way of conducting a romance, and though I never thought I was doing anything immoral (I'd noted in my diary, heavily underlined, Nietzsche's "What is done out of love always takes place beyond good and evil"), we wouldn't have dreamed of openly living together. There was always a certain amount of necessary subterfuge, outsitting his family when I visited him on the Cape, sneaking into his hotel when he came to New York, dodging his nosy old Irish landlady when I stayed in his rooms in Cambridge. Marriage would have solved these problems, but neither of us thought marriage was necessary or feasible. There was no family money on either side to stake a domicile, and, more importantly, we were each involved in our separate academic pursuits. Sean was paving his way for the future at Harvard, class of '50, and I was digging away as a literature major at Bennington, class of '49. It was an absorbing experience for me, and knowing Sean, who delighted in my new-found intellectual interests, heightened it. (Now there was more to talk about than ever, and our letters were crammed with passionate longings to be in bed together mixed with ongoing debates as to the merits of Wolfe, Melville, etc.)

The Bennington system, working in small classes and tutorials, offered a very personal kind of education and one that I found far more rewarding than the mass-oriented, blue-book world of Berkeley. Art, literature, music, philosophy, dance were interrelated, not segregated, and they were to be lived, not surveyed. There was no feedback, no quoting the professor or shoveling out, chapter and verse, the worthy written word which was perfectly available first hand in books. Dostoevski was to be devoured, but that wasn't enough; one had to dig for the quintessential pith and then interpret and evaluate it with original insights and exposition. Eschew the obvious, avoid the cliché, relate, corroborate, extrapolate, do your own thinking. These were the tools, the techniques, for learning what the college catalogue described as an education for "the productive life."

That concept wasn't a shibboleth. It was the criterion of success in one's work and, in broader terms, provided a precept for living. Keep digging for the essence, keep trying to relate, act in terms of the essential. That's what I really learned at Bennington, and as a precept it worked for a long time in an easy, positive way—Sean and the children were the vital elements, love the essence, everything else was minor. Later, when our world fell apart and there were no guidelines, only negatives, it kept me from giving up. I did what I thought I had to do, and it was agonizing; but I never wanted to stop loving Sean, and in the end, when love was all that was left, it was our love that assuaged the pain.

But in the beginning the productive-life principle simply reinforced our relationship. I took a course with Erich Fromm and learned that work and love were the tickets, the means of being productive, and that's what we were doing, working and loving. Marriage could wait, even though it meant there was never enough time together.

What time there was we stretched to the limit, staying up until dawn and, five or six hours later, bounding back for the day. Neither of us was a sleeper—that was secondary—and we refueled ourselves on the high of being together, supplemented by physical activity during the day—energy creates energy—and at night by beer or, when we could afford it, booze. We liked to drink, were good drinkers, hollow-legged, seasoned members of a generation for whom drinking was the name of the game.

My earliest recollection of alcohol was that Prohibition, which ended when I was seven, had been bad, and drinking, in so far as it concerned my parents and their friends, was what grownups did to have fun and hence was socially desirable, *pour le sport.* There was no alcoholic education program in school, and other than the woman who lived next door, I grew up with no personal acquaintanceship with alcoholics, only a vague awareness that there were problem drinkers (and an equally vague notion that Alcoholics Anonymous was the problem drinkers' problem-solver). I assumed that alcoholics came from the very rich or the very poor, people who were so bored or so desperate that they turned to drink for solace. Naturally I had seen the film *The Lost*

Weekend, but I was in my early teens, and though I cried for Ray Milland, it was hard to believe that an otherwise normal guy would lug a typewriter for blocks just to get the price of a drink. The scenes of his writhing in agony with the d.t.'s were frightening but more in the realm of fantasy than fact. The pink elephants that festooned cocktail napkins and invitations were fat, frisky little creatures, not demons. And in other movies getting high meant getting happy. It also meant glamour—Carole Lombard or Cary Grant or Robert Young sipping champagne on sleek ocean liners or fast trains or beautiful country estates—and if Ingrid Bergman got smashed, or Theodora went wild, it was always done with great *élan.* The mean or stupid or morose drunks were dirty cowboys or savage Indians or Victor McLaghlen as an informer, bad guys, none of whom had anything to do with my middle-class life. The literature I read later painted a truer picture. The Consul in *Under the Volcano,* Huck Finn's mean, dirty Pap, Dostoevski's wheedling or driven drunks, they were better drawn and much more real to me, and in a sense they prepared me for what was to happen. But until it happened, they remained characters in books, bigger than life and with no relevance to mine.

Sean told me he didn't drink hard liquor until he went overseas at nineteen. I started earlier. At fifteen I had my first Old Fashioned, served at home to add a festive note before Christmas dinner, and at sixteen, when I began to date, I began to drink. The war was on, and everyone was whooping it up, saying goodbye to those who were drafted or celebrating someone's acceptance in the Air Corps or the Marines. At first one drink, and then two, lasted a whole evening, but by the time I was at Berkeley and having a ball with my ensigns and jg's, getting high was the normal and expected part of the evening's fun. And it didn't matter what kind of rotgut we drank, two-day-old Sonoma Valley Scotch, syrupy Southern Comfort, anything would do as long as it was lethal.

When the war ended and the veterans went back to college,

they were, as I discovered at Williams, seasoned drinkers, not fledglings. Beer was consumed by the bucketful, Scotch and martinis were the status cup and milk punch the Sunday-afternoon supplement. Sean's 1947 Williams yearbook was laced with pictures of drinking parties, students waving bottles, deliberately looking crocked, and comments on individuals' drinking abilities. (Those who got sick and barfed were said to "go praying at the hopper.") The revived racoon-coat spirit of Williams was, to my relief, considerably tempered at graduate school—the parties were smaller, the company more select, the conversation more serious—but the alcohol consumption remained high. Unlike our generation's sons and daughters, who were to withdraw into private pot reveries, drinking was the convivial thing to do. No one was in revolt. Graduate school was the place to be so that one could make it big in the big outside world, and getting there was half the fun. Sean's friends were usually the bright boys in the class, not the playboys, but neither were they the solitary grinds. Those were the CCNY types or the ones from Keokuk, the hinterlands. It was we WASPs who did the drinking, not out of boredom or apathy but because it was the life style and we knew we had it made.

For Sean and his friends, HLS, class of '50, making it had one meaning—joining the Establishment. The Establishment was the elite, the control, the corpus that made the system work, and the system, whether it pertained to law or politics or medicine or the academic world, was, *de facto*, the structure to be maintained. The student protests, civil-rights marches, antiwar demonstrations of the Sixties were unknown in the Forties, and the only campus radicals I knew were a few rich Bennington girls flailing away with an intellectual meat ax at the capitalistic society that supported them. It wasn't a question of being hidebound conservatives; none of us believed there were Commies under every bed, and we all believed in progress, in change. But it was change within the system, not outside it; one could shake it but not, as was to happen fifteen years later, break it or break out of it. It never occurred to Sean and his classmates to go crusading, to practice storefront law in the ghetto, to turn their backs on the big time. The only acknowledged way to make one's mark was within the structure, and the goal was the Establishment.

Making it was important to Sean. Neither of us was the real WASP, of the prep-school-educated, family-financed set for whom security was a birthright, and success, given the necessary brain power, a programmed-in continuum of affluence. I was where I was more or less by happenstance and Sean through a combination of brains and determination. In our marathon night talking sessions I learned that if I had grown up feeling I was a loner, he had grown up feeling he'd been gypped.

The first thirteen years of his life had been a paradigm of all that mine was not. His parents had a blissfully happy marriage, four bright, healthy children, of which he was the oldest, a permanent home, one of the nicest in the small New England town where he lived, and an established role in the community. Being Catholic, they didn't qualify for WASPdom, but everything else was going for the security of the image.

Sean's grandfather, a strapping Irishman who had started as a fifteen-year-old laborer, had built a small domain: land, houses, a lumberyard, oil, gas, ice, property, and business worth half a million dollars; and Sean's father was the heir apparent. He was the younger of two brothers and generally acknowledged to be smarter, shrewder, and far more likable than his older brother, George; and as Grandpa grew older, he turned the business over to Sean's father and left George to do the back-office work.

When Grandpa died it was found that he had left no will. But that was all right. Everything went to his widow, who continued to bake beans on Saturday, go to Mass on Sunday (Grandpa had built the church and given the land), and tend to her chickens and cows, leaving all business details to her younger son. And then, one summer day in his thirty-third year, the heir apparent went off to a clambake, a political get-together, and when he came home he went straight to bed, saying he felt sick to his stomach. He never awakened, and overnight the young prince's family became the poor relations. Uncle George took over the business. This put him in control of Sean's family's purse strings, and smarting from years of running a poor second to his younger brother, he cut his widowed sister-in-law down to size by giving her twenty dollars a week. That, with free fuel, plus free milk and eggs and butter from the farm, was it. The security and happiness were wiped out. Sean's adored father was gone, his mother was sad and lonely, and now every cent counted.

Nonetheless, Sean knew he was the real prince's son, and he set out to prove it. It was just as his Philadelphia grandfather wrote to him shortly after the death of his father:

> Bear in mind that your mother is depending on you to show the way to others. Your future depends in a great measure upon your scholastic showing. Not entirely, of course, but you have the aptitude for learning and a strong will and character and you are liable to go places, places unattainable by either of your grandfathers or your father.

So he made all A's in school, captained the football team, was elected class president year after year, made extra money working for his uncle in the icehouse or lumberyard, and he did it all with grace and skill, and everyone in the family was very proud of him, even his crude, stingy uncle. However, his uncle didn't admire him to the extent of forking out money for college, so at sixteen Sean won a scholarship to Williams. He made good grades, joined a fraternity, played freshman football, earned money by waiting on tables and washing bottles in the lab at night, and, ever mindful of his larger responsibilities, continued to "show the way" to his siblings. He wrote home to his brother:

I had a wonderful time during House Parties. Claude Thornhill played Friday night and was perfect, and the next night there was a big party at the House. What a wild time!

I've had some lucky breaks (remember—*you* make the breaks—nobody hands them to you) and I'm going to college at almost no expense to Mother and having a wonderful time at that. If I can do it, so can you.

A confident, responsible, inspirational message; no complaints. Yet all the while, as he later told me, he resented being a poor boy in a rich boy's school. It was one more hurdle to overcome, not a big one, but not a necessary one either. Had Uncle George not been such a bastard—he had proceeded surreptitiously to transfer title to most of Grandpa's property to his own name—there would have been enough to go around. Sean hated his uncle, but more than that he felt he had been given the shaft by fate, gypped out of his due, and though he was determined to succeed, success couldn't wipe out the anger.

I couldn't really understand the depth of his bitterness— especially since he had done so well on his own—and sometimes it worried me. It almost seemed that he fed on it, deliberately keeping the sore open, gnawing at it, and in my naïveté, knowing nothing of psychiatry and the inner recesses of the mind, I tried to argue that what had happened had happened, that it was the future that mattered, not the past, and that it was love that made the world go round, not money.

"Oh, is that so?" he retorted, grinning. "Then let's make love. Anything to keep you innocent." He leaned over me, nose to nose, eyes to eyes, and said in an amused but serious voice, "You really are a baby when it comes to the real world. That's why you need me, isn't it? To protect you."

Having grown up foraging for myself, I liked being treated as his cherished little cupcake and I enjoyed his protectiveness. But it was an aspect of his personality that bothered me. Sean was extremely possessive. If I was preoccupied, he wanted to know why; if I left the room, he wanted to know wherefore; and as far as other men were concerned, he was always on the edge of jealous anger. When all was going well, as it usually was, his possessiveness made me feel very close to him. But at times I felt too close, engulfed. Whereas I was inclined to stand back, to shore up my defenses, he left himself wide open, quick to laugh, and laugh until the tears rolled down his cheeks, but equally quick to bare his wounds and show his hurt or anger. He was supersensitive to my every mood, almost as if he were trying to make himself vulnerable, and this in turn made me feel vulnerable too, unwittingly both slayer and victim, with too much power and too little control over his emotions. I could give and give, but there was a final nonnegotiable part of me that I had to save for myself, a sense of my own being, but Sean wanted that too. He wanted all of me, all of the time, and if I made an offhand remark that was in any way critical of him (it was fine to disagree intellectually, and in this area he was completely objective and judicious), I never knew when I'd strike a raw chord, and he wouldn't let the remark go until I had explained exactly what I had meant and why. This kind of possessiveness, an insistent need for me to identify with him, sometimes made me recoil, and twice during our five-year courtship I said goodbye forever, only to find that time without him was desolate, boring, and unbearable. Other men were pale by comparison, without his strong commitment to life. Sean had always gone after what he wanted, and I told myself that if possessiveness was part of the package, a cofactor of his intensity and drive, then I would be possessed.

The longest and best time we had together was the summer of 1949. I had graduated, and with money he'd made as a bartender the previous summer we went to Europe for three glorious months, starting off with a month in Paris, staying in a little hotel near Saint-Germain-des-Prés. It was a wonderful time to be there, before the tremendous influx of American tourists, and Paris was friendly, fascinating, uncrowded, and inexpensive. Our room was

21

three dollars a night, and though it had no bath, it had a balcony where we often sat until dawn, sipping wine, listening to the night sounds of the narrow streets—a late-returning reveler, an early-rising shopkeeper—watching the sun come up over the soft pinkish-gray roofs, talking and talking, still trying to get it all said. We were inveterate sightseers: every museum, the law courts, the opera, theater, parks, living on the cheap but splurging when necessary—drinks at the Ritz Bar, dinner at Lapin Agile—endlessly happy to wander the streets and sit for hours at the Deux Magots or Flore (thrilled to behold Sartre doing the same). We went on to the French Alps, picking up with the natives on the strength of Sean's fluent French, hiking with them through the mountains by day in search of panoramas and *fraises des bois,* and at night staying in bed, reading because there was nothing better to do on the chilly nights in the tiny town of St. Pierre de Chartreuse (where I had my first taste of that delicious liqueur). Sean had brought along one battered suitcase full of books, tied together with a rope, to complete his self-scheduled summer reading program, and we had one other that contained our clothes. We visited families he had met during the war in Holland and Belgium—he wanted me to see where he had fought, but all I could see were fields—and we walked the cliffs of the Normandy coast and bicycled the Riviera and fell in love with Giotto in Florence and Harry's Bar in Venice. Sometimes we traveled with various classmates of Sean's from Harvard. The unconventionality of the two of us traveling together—it simply wasn't done in those days among college kids—usually made them feel a bit awkward, but we tried to put them at ease by pretending to have separate rooms. The only hotels that looked askance at our separate passports were those in London, so we left that city after a few days and stayed in a boarding house run by a liberated innkeeper in Cambridge, where we rented a student's suite that was full of books on Russia.

I had never been so happy and wrote long, breathless letters home to my mother, always careful to shield the fact that we were living together. Both of our mothers disapproved of our unconventional ways. Sean began his first postcard home, "Guess who's popped up in Paris?"

When the summer ended, Sean returned to law school and I to New York and job-hunting. We had discussed the idea of getting married and of my working in Boston but mutually discarded it; we had just had a fabulous three-month prehoneymoon, and neither of us had a cent to spend on a wedding. He felt he needed the time alone for a final year's study push, after which he hoped to work in New York, and as my sister, Pat, was now engaged, I was looking forward to moving in with her for a last sister-time together.

I had adored the hotels in Europe, and so, largely for atmospheric reasons, having long since decided that God never intended me to be a serious career woman, I walked into the Plaza Hotel one day, introduced myself to the head of Public Relations, and was hired as his assistant. It was a fun job. I felt like Eloise come of age, and whenever Sean came to New York we celebrated with drinks at the Oak Bar and dining and dancing in the Rendezvous Room, happily living it up on my 50-percent-discounted bill.

That February he made me a valentine. The cover was bright red with a big white heart pasted in the center and, surrounding it, picture cut-outs of a busty cheerleader, beer cans, baby bottles, and champagne glasses. On the inside there were mock-ups of legal documents declaring his love, and on one page he had written, "Not being able to say what I must, I call upon the crystallized wisdom of the ages." And then this by Ezra Pound:

> The tree has entered my hands,
> The sap has ascended my arms,
> The tree has grown in my breast——
> Downward,

> The branches grow out of me, like arms.
> Tree you are,
> Moss you are,
> You are violets with wind above them.
> A child—*so* high—you are,——
> And all this is folly to the world.

I treasured my valentine. Of all the poems he could have quoted, this one said it best. We were our own world, the only world I had ever wanted. I knew I had loved him since the womb, and there would never be anything I could do about this overriding fact.

In June he graduated from law school and in late summer went to work as an associate in a first-rate, medium-sized Wall Street law firm, and the following May 1951—to my parents' great relief—we were properly married in *The New York Times*, with a wedding at St. Patrick's, a reception at the Plaza, and a three-week honeymoon in Bermuda. I wrote more breathless letters to my mother:

Dearest Mama,

This is *heaven* down here. We have a charming cottage built right on a ledge over the ocean which, rain or shine, is the most glorious blue/green I've ever seen— we were in it five minutes after we arrived. Flowers are everywhere, pink oleanders, hibiscus, lilies, etc., etc., plus birds, crickets, green lizards, and we're having a divine time, devoting a great deal of it to sleeping and eating and talking about how wonderful it all is—the martinis are masterpieces and only 50¢—and taking midnight swims and playing tennis and riding bikes.

Sean is great fun and I love him dearly—he looks wonderful with a tan—and I'm awfully happy about being married, though I still flinch when called "Mrs.," as if I were down here under false pretenses. However, since

I've already gotten used to the ring, I suppose I will to the name, shortly.

And, Mama, thank you for being so wonderful about everything for so long. It was all worth it because Sean and I are so happy.

Your darling daughter, B.

When the honeymoon was over, we returned to New York and set up housekeeping in Sean's apartment, one room and kitchen on the ground floor of a brownstone in the East Fifties. The bathroom was down the hall, shared with another tenant, and this was the cause of our first marital argument. Before marriage I found the apartment amusing and cozy, very identifiably Sean's concept of decor. He was one for making do, covering a ramshackle table with a piece of fabric, improvising bookcases out of boards and bricks. Except for the new queen-sized bed we'd bought (this took up a third of the space), it was furnished with gleanings from the Salvation Army and pieces from his Cambridge days. Now that it was my home and not just a trysting place, I began to find it cramped and depressing, and I hated the idea of sharing a bath with a stranger.

I didn't want to start married life complaining and I tried to be a good sport about it, but by the middle of hot, sticky August (with no cross-ventilation the one room was stifling, and after making love we were wringing wet, which meant a trip down the hall to the shower), I told Sean I thought we should look for an apartment with a bath. He was taken aback, somewhat miffed, and said it was a great buy for sixty-five a month. I had always known he was cautious about money, ever careful to check a bill and count the change, but as I, too, was working and contributing to our expenses, I'd assumed he wouldn't feel so pinched. I pointed this out, but he remained adamant, saying sixty-five was all we could afford. I wondered if I had married a selfish tightwad and, worse, if I had totally lost control of my life by getting married.

"You always seem to have money to spend on things you think are important," I said.

"Such as?" he countered.

"Books . . . more and more books, when you already have an overflow." (He was an omnivorous reader, and they were stacked all over the apartment.)

"And what else?" he asked testily.

I couldn't think of anything else except the trips and things that included me, so I returned to the subject of the bathroom, saying that I always felt I was in there on borrowed time, that the other tenant didn't keep it clean, and there was no reason why I should be cleaning up after a stranger and that Sean should be more considerate of my feelings. He said that I should be more considerate of his financial position and that we'd move when he'd decided we could afford to move and, closing the subject, picked up his book and resumed reading.

It flashed through my mind that getting married had been a terrible mistake, that I should have known that he was high-handed, too bossy, and, without a clue as to where I was going to go at nine o'clock on a sweltering night, picked up my purse and went to the door, announcing grimly that I was not going to live in a slum.

"Don't you dare go out that door," he said angrily, springing out of the sagging upholstered chair and grabbing my arm. "You're my wife and you're not leaving."

"I'll do as I damn well please. I'm not your chattel," I said, fighting back tears. Women's Lib was unknown to me then, but even if it had been a familiar cause, I wouldn't have qualified. I hated fighting, always had; I wanted to think of my husband as my shining prince. But now I was fighting with him and my marriage was shattered and I felt utterly defenseless.

"Oh for Christ's sake, darling," he said, wrapping me in his arms, "I know you're not my chattel. All I meant was that I love you and I want to take care of you forever and ever. I'll get you a bathroom, a hundred bathrooms, you'll live like a bloody princess. . . . But just give me a little time."

I said I didn't want to live like a princess and all I wanted was one bath, not a hundred, and then we both started to laugh and suddenly I felt immensely reassured, both about my marriage and my bathroom. A few days later Sean called me up at work to ask if I wanted to look at an apartment in Tudor City, a sublet, ninety a month, nicely furnished, with a living room, bedroom, and bath.

About the time we moved in I found, to our mutual joy, that I was pregnant. Sean said he hoped it would be a boy, and since that's what he wanted, that was what I wanted too. Being pregnant made me love him more than ever, and when baby Sean was born in 1952, it seemed the happiest day of my life.

Twenty-two months later we had another beautiful baby boy, Curtis. Whereas Sean had been a demanding infant, always hungry (I thought he had colic, but the pediatrician said he was just hungry and I should get him on a schedule), Curtis was the soul of cooperation, a gentle, smiling, happy baby. Now we were a real four-cornered family; Papa Bear, Mama Bear, and the two little Baby Bears would grow up together, learning to share, to be pals, and we as parents wouldn't have to worry about a lonely or spoiled only-child. We moved to a two-bedroom apartment, a walk-up off East End Avenue, bought our own furniture, and though life was a bit hectic—Sean worked late many nights, and my days were crammed with mothering—it was full of joy. Marriage, which hadn't seemed so important before the fact, turned out to be the ultimate experience.

Onward and Upward

1954–1961

Living together, knowing that each day would begin and end in each other's arms, solved all the problems. And also the sorrows. In the third year of our marriage Sean's mother died and the next year mine. My mother died slowly and painfully of cancer and Sean's suddenly of a concussion.

Other than the woman who lived next door when I was a child, the only other alcoholic I'd personally known was my mother-in-law. I didn't know about her problem until after we were married. I never really understood why Sean hadn't told me. I accepted the fact that he hadn't because he was perhaps ashamed. A month after we returned from our honeymoon we made a surprise visit to her home one weekend to find her lying in bed, drunk and incoherent. My husband called the family doctor, an elderly, gruff man who clomped upstairs to her bedroom, bellowing, "If you don't stop this foolishness, we're going to put you in the state institution, cockroaches and all."

As shocked as I was to find my nice, ladylike mother-in-law drunk, I was even more shocked by the contemptuous way the doctor treated her, almost as if she were a bum. We took her to a pleasant-looking, small sanitarium for a two-week drying-out period and Antabuse treatment. This was the first time I'd heard of Antabuse, a drug which, when taken with alcohol, makes the drinker violently ill. As I understood it at the time, my mother-in-law's drinking problem was to be resolved by conditioning her, in some abstruse Pavlovian way, to take Antabuse whenever she felt she had to have a drink.

Unfortunately the treatment didn't do much good, but since we lived two hundred miles away and she made a great effort to be sober when we were together, it was by and large an out-of-sight, out-of-mind problem for me. I had only one run-in with her. Using the time-honored American Plan, we left our adored first-born, year-old Sean with her while we went off with friends on a three-day cruise to Nantucket, returning to find our darling staying with my husband's aunt and my baby-sitting mother-in-law dead drunk in bed.

I was livid—totally incapable of understanding her irresponsible act—and stayed on in her house only because it was Sean's vacation and we had no money to go elsewhere. And also because I didn't want his mother to become an issue between us. He said it wouldn't happen again, and then we both dropped the subject; and thereafter he rarely mentioned it except to say that it wasn't her fault, that she had been a wonderful mother but she had had a sad and lonely life since being widowed when he was thirteen.

But once, when she called him on the phone late one night, obviously very drunk, he said in a tense, almost angry voice, "I don't see how she can go out and buy that first bottle—once she does that, it's all over." (And somehow, twelve years later, as if he had never said it, he couldn't stop going out and buying that first daily bottle; it was just as my alcoholism literature said: 40 percent of alcoholics are children of alcoholics.)

Three weeks after Curtis was born, she fell backward down the cement stairs leading to the basement from her kitchen, leaving a half-empty bottle on her sink. She died three days later, and at first Sean was frantic with grief. He stayed up all night, drinking, weeping, raging over his mother's lost and lonely life, cut off in a paroxysm of anguish, and there was no way to reach out to him, to comfort him. Then he was himself again, and after the funeral he said, gently and sadly, "Well, at least I won't have to worry about her drinking any more." The problem was over.

The following year my mother's long suffering with cancer ended, but unlike Sean I was numb with grief, wooden, and I lay in bed that night hollow-eyed. Sean was very tender, telling me of the Catholic doctrines of death and transfiguration, speaking of the body as the temple of the soul, and softening the stark image of my mother's rigid, dead face. He held me, kissing my hair, gradually caressing me to love, and afterward the tears came and I began to weep loose my sorrow. I clung to him, knowing that I needed to love as much as I needed to be loved and that the need to love my mother would be a part of my loving Sean.

The next year we had another baby boy, Nicholas. We hadn't really planned to have Nicholas, but he too was beautiful and we were very pleased with our little surprise package. I was a baby-nut, a breast-feeder, hugger, patter, rocker, anything to keep them healthy and happy, and Sean, though never a diaper changer, was a very affectionate and responsible father.

He spent time with his children, more than most fathers I knew. He said he wanted them to grow up being sure of themselves, to know how to stand their ground and not be pushed around, and he treated each as a very special individual. This way of looking at things didn't include being spoiled or overly aggressive, a bad guy; Sean believed good guys finished first, not last. It meant doing one's best, not quitting, not giving up, and Sean's bedtime stories always concerned the amazing adventures—real cliff-hangers—of highly principled characters such as Tonto and the Lone Ranger or Crusader Rabbit, battling against near insurmountable odds to achieve total, righteous victory. Meeting the challenge head on was a deeply held conviction and was one of the reasons he liked sports so much.

Sean was a very physical man. He relished the cold, tingling ocean, the icy slopes, the rough and tumble of football; and he spent time with his children, city weekends in the park and during his summer vacation, imbuing them with his enthusiasm. He was cautious about safety, but he encouraged them not to be fearful, to play the game for the fun of it—he was very big on razzle-dazzle—and with a touch of the will to win. The boys responded wholeheartedly, and when they were old enough for summer day camp each won numerous awards, not just for athletic skills but also for leadership and good citizenship.

As a disciplinarian, Sean, I found, was extraordinary. Whereas my strong suits were patience and understanding (which, after a point, became a do-it-because-I-said-to-do-it ultimatum), he ameliorated problems more readily. I used to watch in wonder as he moved in swiftly and decisively, bending or kneeling to be on an eye-to-eye level, and in a matter of minutes he had changed a negative attitude into a positive one. There was no way on earth I could get baby Nicholas to take medicine, even a pulverized aspirin; no matter how I disguised the taste, out of his mouth it would come in an enraged and spattering spew. Yet Sean could always talk him into swallowing it, with Nicholas acting as if he were pleased to be doing Daddy a great personal favor. I suppose it was a kind of discipline by charisma, with Sean using his innate optimism and enthusiasm to persuade and woo the children to his point of view. Whatever it was, it worked, and our children weren't whiners or spoilsports and, though prone to roughhouse, they rarely came to blows. They were good-looking little boys (I dressed them in matching Best & Company seersuckers and corduroys), strong and sturdy, and everyone said they favored their father—especially the eldest, Sean, who from the day he was born was, in appearance and temperament, a decided chip off the old block. As young Sean grew, the resemblance continued, all of which gave his father an amused but glowing sense of immortality.

These were glowing years. I had found my niche in life as Sean's wife, and he was ambitiously pursuing his in the career world. After four years of corporate practice on Wall Street he left in 1954 for two years' intensive litigation experience as an Assistant United States Attorney for the Southern District of New York, hitting his stride and sometimes the front pages as a criminal prosecutor. He was active in the Young Republican movement and, curious for a look behind the scenes in the Eisenhower Administration, went to Washington in the late spring of 1956 as an assistant to the General Counsel in the Defense Department. (He had always been keenly interested in government policy, and once, at a party at Harvard when life goals were being discussed, Sean had said he'd like to be Secretary of State. "Why not the President?" someone asked flippantly. "The office is too political. I'm more interested in working for viable international relations than in vote-getting," he answered.) He said we'd stay only a year, time to get the feel of the administration. We had a pleasant time (he found us a nice house in Georgetown at a remarkably low rent) and met congenial people, but we missed New York life. And there was another reason to return.

The year before, in 1955, we'd bought a house in East Hampton, a small country inn surrounded by potato fields and only a two-minute walk to the ocean. To help pay expenses I continued the summer-inn operation, which meant I had to be there while Sean worked in the city. Getting to East Hampton on the tip of Long Island was a three-hour drive or train ride from New York but an impossible weekend commute from Washington, time-consuming and expensive. We adored the house and the area, and after one harried summer of truncated Friday-midnight-to-Sunday-afternoon weekends, we decided Washington would have to get along without us. I had a party just before we left, and, to my astonishment and embarrassment, Sean suddenly seemed very drunk, almost on the verge of passing out at dinner. Then he sobered up, just as quickly, at least enough to make it through the rest of the evening. I dismissed the incident as one that could and did happen to anyone in our heavy-drinking society.

In the fall of 1957 he joined one of the largest and most prestigious law firms on Wall Street, a firm with over a hundred lawyers, one of the ultimate sanctuaries of the legal establishment. He told me that it was unusual for a firm such as this to hire an "outsider" as an associate, the usual course being to start after graduating from law school and then to stay on for ten years, by which time one was either made a partner or one moved out. He had been brought in to work on a particular litigation case, an antitrust suit, to be argued before the Supreme Court. He said he knew it was risky, that his future there could well depend on whether or not the firm won its case, but he had turned down other offers in smaller firms where a partnership was almost guaranteed because this firm was the real Establishment, and though the ultimate achievement, a partnership, was iffy, he was within the gates.

"I've been lucky so far," he said quietly, modestly, but with pride, referring to the fact that without either wealth or connection—not prerequisites to making it but certainly helpful factors —he had moved, step by step, from being a poor, small-town boy to the big time.

Back in New York, we moved into the rent-controlled six-room apartment Sean had found, just off Park and within walking distance of the private school where young Sean and Curtis were enrolled with partial scholarships. The New York parental private-school hysteria was already in full flower, and this school was one of the most difficult in the city to crash, but four-year-old Curtis proved to have highly desirable test scores. I told the admissions director they couldn't have Curtis without taking Sean, Jr. (she'd said his grade level was filled), because, with an eighteen-month-old baby at home, I couldn't be picking up and delivering at two separate schools. The director suddenly found that there was room for Sean after all, so that problem was solved; and aside from the discombobulations of mixing my husband's demanding career with three growing children, a busy social life, a summer of inn-keeping, life was just the way we thought it ought to be. Looking back, perhaps we did too much, but at the time it worked, and the center held with the help of two tension-breakers—sex and alcohol. **1789671**

From the very beginning we had made love whenever and wherever we could: beds, boats, cars, trains, meadows, mornings, afternoons, and nights. During our five-year affair the only stumbling block had been social conventions, finding a secret time and place, but that had gone away with marriage. However, as we became a growing family and were no longer a couple, another problem loomed: time, not secret time, but just time itself. After the second baby was born, and then the third, it seemed that as a group they never got any older, and between the endless distractions they presented and the rigors of the working day, it was hard to find uninterrupted time when we weren't exhausted. Locking the bedroom door couldn't lock out the sound of a crying baby or a four-year-old flooding the tub or hammering with blocks, and by late evening we were too stunned to do much more than fall asleep in each other's arms. We decided it was well worth the expense to hire a baby-sitter on weekends and during Sean's vacation because a life without loving wasn't living. Sex was a vital means of rising above the mundane aspects of marriage, the endless shopping, cooking, cleaning, bill-paying; in addition to the physical satisfaction, it gave us our own adult identity distinct from the children. We were a family, yes, but we were more than that; we were lovers, and we treated each other as such, eschewing sarcasm or vituperation or speciousness. I couldn't have stood a marriage in which there was constant in-fighting, and though we had our disagreements—he said I was too much of a patsy for the children, and I sometimes accused him of leaving his clothes around, as if I were his valet—they were simply that and not bitter quarrels. We agreed on the basics and the rest was peripheral. He managed the money, I managed the children and home, and we mutually managed our social and recreational life, and if there was a conflict of interest, we hashed it out then and there.

I recall one occasion when we had planned to go skiing, but nine-month-old Nicholas came down with a bad cold, and I couldn't get the regular baby-sitter, so we decided Sean should go and I'd stay home. When he returned Sunday evening, beaming and exhilarated, I met him at the door half-crackers from having spent the weekend inside with a five- and a three-year-old and a perpetually crying baby. As he put down his skis, I shoved my little screamer into his arms, saying, "Here—you listen to him for a while—I'm going out."

After hearing out my ten-minute harangue on my horrible weekend, Sean grinned, put his free arm around me, baby Nicholas miraculously shut up, and the experience no longer seemed so horrendously devastating. At any rate, it was over. Sean was back home, and though the day had been interminable, it was now evening and time to have a drink.

If there was any sluice gate needed in our marriage, it was the nightly ritual of cocktails. This was the reward time.

We felt we owed ourselves the pleasure and peace of the cocktail hour, a chance to communicate as civilized adults rather than merely as parents and drones. By the time Sean came home at seven, the children were bathed and fed, and while they played or did homework, we renewed ourselves over our nightly drinks. I was worn down from a long day of mothering; he was keyed up from a long day of working, and this was the time to shift into a mutually compatible gear and pull our separate pursuits into a shared perspective. We loved gin martinis, and with the first cool, clean, bracing, embracing sip, the accumulated tensions of the day magically began to melt away. We had another drink or so after the children were in bed and then an *intime* dinner around nine. (Even if Sean had come home in time to eat with the children, which he almost never did, we were against the idea, except on holidays; we gave a great deal of ourselves to the children, but the dinner hour was for relaxing and not for dodging spilled milk.) After dinner we read until it was time to turn on the eleven-o'clock news on the TV set in our bedroom. The evenings flew by, and though we went out fairly often, dinner and cocktail parties and the theater, it was just as nice to stay home, still happy as clams at high tide in our still-private world.

Although my husband had been brought up a Catholic and believed it to be the one true church, he was not much of a churchgoer and never pressed for my conversion. The only demands he had made were to be married by a priest and to raise the children as Catholics, and, to satisfy the nuptial requirements, I had taken instructions prior to our wedding. I made a sincere attempt to understand the Catholic religion, but having dropped out of the Episcopal Church in my late teens because the doctrine seemed untenable, I found the Catholic dogma even more abstruse. However, after our third son, Nicholas, was born, and even though I couldn't accept the taboos on birth control and divorce, I went back for further instructions and one morning went quietly off by myself to a nearby Jesuit church and became a convert. It wasn't a decision based on reason or a commitment that hinged on understanding. It was simply that I didn't know what I had done to deserve such a good life, and I believed I owed God thanksgiving.

I liked going to Mass on Sunday. It gave me a feeling of peace, a sense of the order of God's love. However, I didn't go to communion because I didn't go to confession. I saw no sense in confessing my practice of birth control each week when I had no intention of giving up my diaphragm.

We had had three babies in the first five years of marriage, and though we adored them, I had had enough of ministering to the needs of an infant at a time when I was also trying to find my way raising the older two, and Sean was deeply involved with his career. It meant that our life *à deux* was pretty much a catch-as-catch-can affair. Now that Nicholas was almost two and his schedule was fairly well synchronized with that of young Sean and Curtis, we had, after seven years of marriage, reached a new plateau. We were in our early thirties, old enough to be somewhat wiser but not so old as to feel aged, and the directions we had been seeking in our twenties had more or less emerged. Sean was where he wanted to be, careerwise, and now that the children were launched, home life was less hectic. Conversion or no, I wanted to keep it that way.

In the early summer of 1958, just before we were to move to East Hampton for the season, I walked glumly to the obstetrician's office to get confirmation of what I already knew was true. Despite the diaphragm, I was pregnant again.

Another baby meant another two years of irregular hours, of less space in the apartment, of more expense—the diaper service, the monthly visits to the pediatrician—of hauling out the baby carriage again and setting off to the park in flotilla formation, Sean, Jr., and Curtis flanking me while I pushed the pram with one hand and clutched Nicholas with the other. It meant less time for myself and less uninterrupted time with Sean. And I was tired of being pregnant. I couldn't wait to start wearing maternity clothes when I was expecting the first baby, but now I loathed them and wondered if, the fourth time around, Sean wouldn't find me a lumbering mess.

He was a very attractive thirty-four-year-old man. My wiry college boy had put on weight and it became him, filled out his strong, athletic body; his hair had turned gray, and in his mid-night-blue or banker's-gray Brooks Brothers suits he had a youthful man-of-distinction look. And his college-boy intensity had mellowed. He was still very direct, but more at ease, more engaging. He liked women and they liked him, and I could even imagine that one day I might have trouble in that department. Instead of racing to telephone him the glorious news, I waited until that evening when we were into our second martini and then stonily made my announcement. Sean winced and took a sip of his drink, a bracer.

"Well, it's not my fault," I said defensively, defiantly. "And I'm the one who'll have to do all the work."

He looked at me and then laughed softly. "I know it's not your fault, darling; don't talk like that. It's because you're my beautiful girl and I'd rather make love to you than anything in the world—so first things first, even if it means another fifty thou to feed and educate the little bastard."

The baby was due the first of the year, so, being immensely pregnant, I didn't go with Sean to his law firm's annual holiday party, an occasion I had always, in the past, found at best a strain. It was a formal reception, a best-foot-forward affair, complete with receiving line and held, traditionally, on New Year's Day, a time when we traditionally had hangovers (New Year's Eve being the traditional time to stay up late drinking). Other than the most senior partners and their wives, they being the apotheosis of the legal profession, everyone present strove mightily to make the right impression—the junior partners on the senior partners, the associates on the junior and senior partners, with the correlative wives performing according to their husband's rank. There was much maneuvering to talk to the right people and say the right things for the right amount of time. One knew when time had run out—perhaps even been overstepped—when the target partner discreetly but decisively glanced away, his face lighting up at the sight of another, and the only graceful way to end a half-finished sentence was with a *non sequitur*, a "Happy New Year" or whatever, and then gracefully peel away and onward. Sean (he being the Establishment-oriented member of the family, not I) thought the receptions were great. I was always careful not to drink too much, to show the proper propriety, but he always drank as usual, and as usual the drinks put him in high, good spirits and he never wanted to leave until the end. However, being about to give birth, I wasn't up to the ordeal of standing by for several hours.

Two days later our fourth son, Seamus, was born. He too was perfect. There was a period of adjustment: young Sean, bumped for the third time from his role of kingpin, told a friend his mother no longer loved him, and though Curtis was very gentle, Nicholas had to be restrained from overly ardent bear hugs. The apartment was definitely more crowded and life more discombobulated, but at the end of three months Seamus was an accepted member of the family, and when he finally reached the more tractable age of two, he became one of the boys, more or less synchronized with their schedules. With a husband I adored, four wonderful sons, an apartment in town, a house in the country (we had given up the inn business), I felt we had reached an even higher plateau.

After ten years of marriage, when we were relaxing over our evening martinis, we'd sometimes say with objective and serene satisfaction, "This is too good—it can't possibly last," absolutely certain we had the best of all possible worlds for as long as we both should live. That was in 1961. Four confused years later the good life was washed out, drowned in bottles of booze, and my warm, wonderful husband had become a dissolute alcoholic.

4

Coming Apart at the Seams

1961-1965

Watching Sean turn into an alcoholic was like witnessing an elusive, ghastly metamorphosis, a freak mutation, a process too complex, too ambiguous and too quick to understand but too frightening to ignore. The manifestations were at first subtle, easy to rationalize, but then they accelerated, and one day he was transformed. He changed physically, emotionally, psychologically. His skin tone changed, his weight, his attitude toward me and the children and his job changed, and the worst of it was that he acted as though he didn't give a damn. Our world was coming apart at the seams and he just went right on drinking. The first morning that I came into the kitchen and saw the gin bottle on the breakfast counter, its contents rocking from side to side, I was thrown into a cold panic, but when I asked him about it that evening, he brushed my question aside and asked if I wanted a martini. I couldn't understand his diffidence, nor could I believe it was deliberate. Vacillating between anger and sorrow, resentment and forgiveness, I was drained by ambivalence and I did nothing. I was totally unprepared for what was happening.

From our very first beer-drinking date onward, drinking was a part of our lives, a fun part. What we considered to be normal drinking patterns in college continued after we were married but on a less frenetic scale. There were cocktail parties and dinner parties, but there were also children and jobs, so we were usually home by midnight, sometimes a bit plastered but more often pleasantly high. (Sometimes we'd say to hell with the baby-sitter and move on to the Stork Club for dancing until three, getting tight when the spirit moved us.) Hangovers were no great problem; we both had a high energy quotient and could get through any day, maybe a little ragged but never undone. If this pattern indicated a proclivity to alcoholism, I wouldn't have known it, because although we drank a lot, so, it seemed, did everyone else of interest. Our best friends were, in the main, our best drinking buddies, not on that basis alone but because they were interesting, stimulating go-getters, out to make their mark on the world and, at the same time, to enjoy it, people who liked to stay up late and talk and drink and weren't afraid to let their inhibitions loose to the winds. We eschewed the company of those continually cautious souls perpetually nagged by their nervous wives to make it an early evening. They lacked our knack for ebullient life.

The ebullient life peaked in 1960, on our second trip to Europe, ten years after our premarital one and, in style, its antithesis. It was a business trip for Sean and three other lawyers, and I joined them in London, from where we moved merrily by jet and limousines to the best hotels and restaurants in Paris, Amsterdam, London, Oslo, and Copenhagen, having a smashing time all the way. We never neglected culture, just gave it shorter shrift, sandwiching museum sorties in between catching planes, conferences, lingering luncheons, and long nights of bubbles and eggs, jeroboams of Moet Chandon and the best and blackest of beautiful, beady caviar.

Everyone was married, but I was the only wife who had been invited to join the pack, and I soon learned why. Two of the lawyers were dashing Wall Streeters, one of whom told his dates he was divorced; the other would solemnly announce that his wife was dead. The third, a bland government lawyer, apparently congenitally content to do without feminine companionship, told me it had never occurred to him to bring his wife along.

It made me feel very special and very secure in our marriage that Sean wanted me along, and living in luxury, without the children to interfere, we reverted to acting like lovers, discovering, among other delights, that it was simply super to bathe together in the pool-sized European tubs. We were terribly pleased with ourselves. I felt attractive and adored and Sean worldly and successful. One day, when we were gluing ourselves back together with a preluncheon Fernet Branca, he said, "You know, I decided I am lucky. Somehow I never thought I'd outlive my father, but I'm three years older than he was when he died and everything is working the way I wanted it to."

Two years after our European trip it gradually began to dawn on me that the ebullient life was getting out of control. We went to a skating party at a club, and after cocktails and dinner everyone stepped out on the rink. Sean, who had learned to skate on the frozen cranberry bogs of New England and could go faster backward than I could forward, kept slipping and sliding, sometimes skidding across the ice on all fours, a slaphappy grin on his face, like a funny clown but not at all funny to me. Our friends tried to act as if it was amusing, helping him to his feet with good-humored grace, but I could tell they were embarrassed for him. And for me, too. I tried to get him to leave, but he persisted in flailing around until, finally, it was closing time and we all left. Riding home in the cab, I asked how he could have gotten so tight. He wouldn't answer and I didn't press. Just one of those things.

But the isolated incidents gained momentum, and more

43

often than not he became not just tight but drunk at parties, especially cocktail parties, where there was no cutoff for dinner. I told myself it was the stress of work, or that since Sean did everything with unusual verve, it followed that he drank with greater gusto. But as we would set forth, I began to ask him, or rather to tell him, to please try to stay sober. And I began to watch him, asking him please not to have another drink and to say we should leave. I didn't like the role of nagging wife, especially because it was to no avail. Occasionally I confronted him with morning-after accounts, telling him he had acted like a damn fool and embarrassed me. He'd either laugh it off—not in his good-humored way but sneeringly—or tell me to go to hell. I didn't like dissension any more than I liked nagging, and since he had never talked to me like this, I'd shut up and skulk away, morose over the cracks that were beginning to seam our private world.

Because the scene was also shifting at home. I tried to tell myself he was the same, sweet husband and father, just a little edgier, maybe nervous. It wasn't like him to snap at me over trivialities, such as the Sunday we took the children to the Central Park Zoo cafeteria for lunch and he barked, "Oh, for Christ's sake, make up your mind," when I paused to debate over a hamburger or a hot dog. And though he had always tried to get exercise in New York, it wasn't like him to call and say he was playing squash and then reel in at ten, stoned. And though our evening ritual of cocktails had been rewarding, watching Sean get drunk was not. He didn't get drunk every night, but when he did it made him too volatile, overly exuberant like the times he'd start a football game with the boys in the living room when it was time for their bed. And sometimes it made him mean.

He came into the kitchen one winter Sunday night when I was serving the children their supper at the breakfast bar. He had started drinking that afternoon as he watched the football game, and he was keyed up, quarterbacking some of the plays. The kitchen was small and, annoyed that he was tight and that he was

44

in the way, I said irritably, "Oh, stop it. . . . Get out of the way."
Sean stopped short, eyes flashing, and pushed me toward the
kitchen window.

"Don't ever talk that way to me. Or out you'll go!"

The children were wide-eyed, aghast, and Curtis, nine,
jumped down from his stool, wedging himself between us. "Don't
hurt Mommy," he said staunchly.

Sean laughed quickly, as if it had been a joke, and I told the
boys to finish their supper, as if the incident were of no consequence; but for a moment my heart beat faster. It was an ugly side
of Sean I never knew existed, and I was afraid, as much for him
as for myself. And then I tried to put it out of my mind, because
most of the time he was his warm, wonderful self and our life
wasn't really different. Or so I told myself. He went to work, I
took care of the house and the children, we laughed and talked
and made love, went on ski weekends with the boys in the winter
and played family tennis on Sunday mornings in the summer; and
on Saturday afternoons in the city we still went to museums and
galleries and to see foreign films. It was just that sometimes Sean
seemed preoccupied, almost depressed, until he had a few drinks.
And then he was his witty, charming, interesting self again—that
is, until he had too many drinks.

He was putting on weight, getting heavier in the middle, but
then so did many men his age. And sometimes he was less than
meticulous in his dress, wearing a shirt that was frayed at the
collar or a suit that should have gone to the cleaners. I mentioned
this a few times when I was sitting in bed, sipping the coffee he
brought me each morning before the children were up, watching
as he dressed. He either reacted petulantly, as if I were deliberately trying to hurt his feelings, or sarcastically, telling me to mind
my own business. I'd put it down to the fact that he probably had
a little hangover and try to say something cozy, like "Your business is my business and mine yours; I thought we agreed on that,"
but it didn't work. It was getting harder to communicate at times.

And that made me sad, bewildered. And the way he was drinking made me embarrassed at parties and uncomfortable at home. And though I tried not to show it, underneath it made me angry. He was letting me down.

It seemed that since he had told me in the spring of 1962 that he had strong doubts about being made a partner in his firm that his drinking had increased. We were sitting in Central Park, watching the boys play baseball, and I remarked that he seemed preoccupied.

"I guess I am," he said casually.

"About what?" I asked.

"About making decisions I don't want to make," he answered obliquely.

"You mean about being made a partner?" I asked tentatively.

"No, about not being made a partner. Let's get the boys and go home," he finished, closing the subject.

Sean's relationship to his law firm had become a difficult matter for us to discuss. (The other taboo subject was his mother's alcoholism. I'd long since given up probing the effect it had on his life, because he cut me off, saying it wasn't really a problem, when I knew from talking to his sister and youngest brother that it definitely was.)

In the monolithic firms such as his, one either made it as a partner or one didn't by the age of thirty-five or so, approximately ten years after law school. If one hadn't received the golden tap by then, and only 20 percent at best did, it was time to move out, either to a client corporation or a small firm or whatever. What one didn't do was to hang around. Hanging around, watching as contemporaries and then younger associates were made partners, was awkward, even humiliating. Looking back, I find it hard to realize that being made a partner was so terribly important, not just to Sean but to our lawyer friends, but that's the way it was in the early Sixties. We had several friends, first-rate attorneys a few years older than Sean, who hadn't made it in their huge firms, and the matter was treated almost as if they had been expelled from school, a distressing turn of events to be spoken of in the most carefully casual way, as if it really didn't matter, when we all knew it was a real blow to one's professional pride.

Sean knew he was taking a risk when he went with the firm and he had told me I had no idea how brilliant some of his associates were. He knew the competition was fierce and he knew it was also, in addition to brains, a question of the luck of the draw, working with the right sympatico partners on the right cases. Nonetheless he had plunged in, with stars in his eyes. He wanted to be a partner—and naturally I wanted it for him—but I didn't know how much it meant until we went to his firm's annual party on New Year's Day in 1962.

Partnerships were announced in December, so in addition to being a formal get-together, the receptions were also a kind of coming-out party for the new members, with the sun of conviviality beamed directly on those who had recently made it. As usual everyone was dressed in his or her conservative best, and as usual the ballroom was festive with red poinsettias and gleaming silver candelabra, and there was much maneuvering to talk to the right person. As soon as we stepped into the room I sensed that we were now in the shadows.

Sean, who was hung over and a little shaky, headed me straight for the bar and, armed with drinks, we began to make the rounds, only to find that after a smiling nod, a few brief words, the target partner would glance away, beaming toward another, the signal that the audience was over. We found ourselves talking to each other, or trying to, and that was more awkward, the whole point being to circulate. I excused myself and went to the ladies room, mainly to get away, and when I returned I didn't see Sean in the crowd and struck off on my own. Conversation was strained, wispy and inconsequential, polite for politeness's sake, and I stopped to chat with a friend whose husband had recently been made a partner. We were fairly good friends, and as I had already offered my congratulations, it was a relief to be talking without trying to make the right impression; but I discovered the competition was inescapable, and now it had a cutting edge. Her husband came rushing up and, ignoring me completely, said with annoyance, "Don't stand there talking to her. I told you to move around."

I went to look for Sean to say I wanted to go home. He was standing alone by the bar, weaving. As I approached he started across the floor and fell. The two partners who helped me get him into a cab were very kind, but nothing they could have done would have eased my mortification. And heartbreak.

I tried to get Sean to talk about it the next day, saying he mustn't take his career so seriously and that with his brains and background there were myriad opportunities, but he wouldn't discuss it. Three months later he eased himself out of Wall Street and into a small, high-powered company as general counsel. He spoke with optimism of his future there, but the first morning he left for his new job he lingered at the door as we kissed goodbye, a rueful little grin playing about his lips, like a boy gamely going about a chore he detested, and six weeks later I came into the kitchen and saw the gin bottle on the breakfast bar, the contents sloshing from side to side.

When he came home that evening I waited until he had changed into his chinos, and then I asked why he was drinking in the morning. He just looked at me and said, as he had for so many years, only this time with more cool than affection, "Would you like to have a martini?"

"No! I would like to know why, why in God's name you're doing this? What's wrong? Is it me? Is it your job?" I wanted to sound calm, reasonable, but I wasn't good at arguing, and the words came too fast and my voice was harsh and I was shaking with rage. "You've got to face up to what you're doing. You know what happened to your mother! She was a drunk, she made your life miserable, but you won't admit it and you won't admit you're messing up our life, because you're just like she was, a selfish, weak, goddam drunken . . ." I didn't finish, because his hand came slamming across my face.

For a moment we stood staring at each other. And then I started to cry, and he put his arms around me, saying over and over he was sorry. It was the first time he had ever hit me, but that wasn't why I was crying. For the first time in my life I had deliberately tried to hurt him, to get back at him, to jab the sore spot of his mother's drinking. It didn't matter that I hadn't really meant to; it was done, and nothing would ever be the same again.

And it wasn't. We had squared off, he in his corner and me in mine, and by the summer of 1963 I could no longer look away and try to pretend that all was the same. We were again caught up in the continual rounds of East Hampton parties, and though it was hard for anyone not to get a little drunk by the end of a three-party night, that was different from getting totally bombed, only to start the day off with a restorative shot of gin in the morning orange juice and then, after tennis, numerous pre-luncheon martinis. A few close friends asked me what the problem was —why did Sean drink so much and why did I put up with it— but I didn't want to talk about it. The questions put me on the defensive. I didn't know why he drank so much, and I put up with it because I didn't know what else to do. He wasn't my child, to be sent off to bed, kept home from the party if he misbehaved. I had loved him because he was his own man, strong and determined, and, drunk or sober, he was still his own man and there was no way to control him. Looking back, I'm sure the questions were meant to be helpful, but at that stage in my life they added to my embarrassment and confusion. In our circle it was okay to get drunk but not to be a drunk, and for what we knew of it alcoholic was only a euphemism for a sloppy, non-self-respecting drunk.

Not knowing where else to turn for help and being a believer in the written word, I decided to go to the small village library in East Hampton and discreetly research the matter. There were three books catalogued under "Alcohol": Marty Mann's *New Primer on Alcoholism,* Berton Roueché's *On Alcohol—The Neutral Spirit,* and Lillian Roth's *I'll Cry Tomorrow.* I chose the *Primer,* which, as stated in the preface, was addressed to those "who have to cope with the alcoholic" as well as the alcoholic himself. And that day, at age thirty-six, I learned for the first time that alcoholism was in no sense a euphemism for drunkenness but a disease unto itself.

The *Primer* was direct and to the point. With impressive exactitude the author estimated the alcoholic population to be "4,712,000" in 1955 and "five millions" in 1958. Making the supposition that each alcoholic affected five people (family, friends, fellow workers), she wrote:

> And that means twenty-five million nonalcoholics directly affected: a grand total that involves over one sixth of our population with alcoholism.
>
> Too many in this great mass of people still do not know the facts about alcoholism or what to do about it. Too many are still hiding, in fear and shame. It is for them I write, to bring them the latest news—the good news about things *that work.*

That was a very positive, reassuring statement. My husband was the core of my life, and I resolved to make the "things that work" work. The opening paragraph of Chapter 1 laid the problem on the line in chilling terms:

> Alcoholism is a disease which manifests itself chiefly by the uncontrollable drinking of the victim, who is known as an alcoholic. It is a progressive disease, which, if left untreated, grows more virulent year by year, driving its victims further and further from the normal world, and deeper and deeper into an abyss which has only two

outlets: insanity or death. Alcoholism, therefore, is a progressive, and often fatal, disease . . . *if* it is not treated and arrested. But it can be arrested.

Insanity? Death? Not my alcoholic. I read until closing time and then checked the book out, determined to follow to the letter and spirit the prescribed methods of help.

In the next few years I was to read many books and tracts written for those who are trying to help and/or cope with an alcoholic, and I still believe the *Primer* is as good, if not better, than most in defining the disease, its progressive stages, and in trying to advise ways of helping recovery. But in so far as helping my alcoholic was concerned, I might as well have confined my reading to Berton Roueché's *On Alcohol—The Neutral Spirit*, a book concerned more with the drink than the drinker.

Reading the *Primer* at home, I learned that *my* attitude was a major, if not *the* major, determinant in his recovery.

There is a great deal the family can do to help the alcoholic make a start toward recovery. Their own attitude toward him and his problem is often the key. And if they are properly informed as to the nature of alcoholism and what it does to the alcoholic, a sympathetic, understanding and constructive attitude should not be too difficult to attain.

A "sympathetic, understanding and constructive attitude." That was the key. The author continued:

There is no question that it will pay dividends for alcoholics generally respond gratefully to warmth and understanding, just as they respond resentfully to what they consider criticism and censure.

There was no question about it. Up until now I had failed Sean, probably made him drink more. Since I loved him, my natural instinct was to be sympathetic and understanding (the second the words had come out of my mouth about his mother I knew I was the guilty party), but heretofore I had been sympathetic and understanding only up to a point. When he got drunk at a family picnic on the beach it was hard to be sympathetic toward him when I could see what he was doing to the children. On one occasion he had lurched over to where Curtis was talking to his friends and unsteadily but persistently tried to spar with the group. To cover his embarrassment, Curtis laughed and said, "Daddy, why do you always drink so much?" Sean suddenly grabbed the Coke out of his son's hand and threw it across the beach, saying, "That will teach you, you little bastard, not to talk to your father that way." I saw the look of anguish on Curtis's face, and he was the one I sympathized with, not Sean. And it was hard to be understanding when he stayed up late, playing records at full blast, when I was trying to sleep; or when he made drunken passes at women, as he had taken to doing. Henceforth, I would try harder.

The big point was to be constructive. Heretofore I had been too wishy-washy, unable to take a firm stand, shifting between anger and sorrow. The *Primer* said I should broach the subject in an objective, general way, as a topic unto itself and "not, of course, pointing out that the person they are talking to is in their opinion an alcoholic." That was difficult, similar to trying to talk about cancer to a cancer patient without making reference to the individual's illness. But it was more than challenging with Sean; it was impossible, because whenever I brought the subject up he pulled down his invisible shade and ignored me or said irritably, "Oh, get off it. I'm bored with your lectures."

I did as my literature suggested and put relevant reading material in an inconspicuous place (the bottom shelf of Sean's bedside table), where he could read it unobserved and without feeling I was accusing him of wrongdoing, but he never touched it. I looked for other guidelines in the *Primer*, but it seemed to me that being constructive was more a matter of what not to do rather than a series of positive steps.

In a chapter entitled "The Home Treatment"—"the methods frequently used by desperate and harassed families who are trying "to bring [their alcoholic] to his senses"—the *Primer* warned against trying to reason the partner into not drinking, making emotional appeals, promising, coaxing, threatening, withholding the bottle or money with which to buy it. Instead, one was to become "properly informed as to the nature of alcoholism and what it does to the alcoholic." And then we were back at the point where a "sympathetic, understanding and constructive attitude should not be too difficult to attain."

I was to read this chapter over and over, as I had the paragraph on colic in Dr. Spock's book on baby care, never quite understanding what it was I was actually supposed to do. In each instance the prime recourse seemed to be to hang in with steely, loving calm until the problem went away. And that's what I tried to do. I tried not to show my anger or resentment when he was drunk, and I tried to make the most of the times when he was sober, but these times were getting fewer and farther between. (The morning shot was now ritual, and he got drunk every night when he came home from work.) But if nothing else, my newfound knowledge about alcoholism helped to keep the peace. If there was no way to reach out to Sean, to crack through his invisible wall, at least the children were spared hearing us argue. That wasn't much, but since I had grown up listening to my own parents fight, it was better than nothing.

And then came the real test. The day was November 22, 1963. President Kennedy had been shot, and Sean came home early from work, almost hysterical with rage, one moment morose and stunned, the next livid with fury at the madness of a world that destroyed Kennedy, like himself a dedicated son of New England and, like himself, a victim of gross irrationality and craven stupidity. I was bewildered, unable to understand how he identified so passionately with a man he had never met, hadn't even voted for, until many martinis later I heard Sean on the phone, reaming out the board chairman of his company, telling him he was a double-dealing bastard. And then I knew. The endless drinks at night, the quick, clandestine shots in the morning, the bloodshot eyes and nervous hangovers were no longer our own little secret. When he hung up the phone I put my arms around him and said, "Oh, darling, we've got to talk about this."

He shook his head. "What's there to say?" he asked.

The unbelievably sad three-day television coverage of the funeral deflected and diminished the shock of Sean's being fired. We all, the children included, just sat and watched, no one saying a word. When it was over, after Arlington, it was as if a catharsis had taken place, a time for sorting out and reaffirming values. Compared to the tragedy of Kennedy's death, being fired no longer mattered, and Sean refused to talk about it, except to say he never should have taken the job in the first place.

The impact of being fired seemed salubrious. He was far less tense and he drank less, sometimes a martini before lunch but no morning shots, and he didn't get drunk every night. I decided that his getting fired had been good for him, shaken him up to the reality of the damage his drinking was doing. I knew also that it was a frightening blow to his ego, one that could readily push him further into alcoholism, and though I tried tactfully to point out that drinking had been a factor, I rationalized that anyone worth his salt and independent views was entitled to being fired once, and the time off would give him a chance to get his bearings. The long-run solution was to get a job more suited to his interests, one that wouldn't necessitate alcohol to drown frustrations. I suggested that maybe we should get out of New York for a while, do something entirely different, join the Peace Corps and live abroad, or even move to East Hampton year round so that he could establish his own independent practice there. He treated these ideas as if I had suggested we move to Mars, reminding me that he was in the top 10 percent of his law class and therefore belonged in New York, where the legal profession was the most stimulating and remunerative. He said he was prepared to sit it out until he found the right slot and for me not to worry, as he had been given almost a year's severance pay and had worked out a deal with his former company by which he would still nominally be general counsel so he wouldn't have to explain his unemployment. And the stock market, which had been bullish for a decade, was still perking along nicely, and Sean had around $60,000 in securities.

We decided not to tell the children that he wasn't working so as not to upset them, and he asked me not to tell friends for professional reasons. And he said he wouldn't start looking until after the first of the year, the holiday season being a hopeless time to research jobs, and his enforced idleness would make it a good time to take us all to Vermont for post-Christmas skiing.

This seemed like a good time to bring up the subject of Alcoholics Anonymous. We had been talking while we were lying in bed, enjoying the luxury of being able to make love in the afternoon while the children were in school, and though the mere mention of AA usually made Sean angry, I felt he was now in a properly receptive mood, as my alcoholism literature recommended. (I'd pursued my reading in New York to learn, again and again, that it was my attitude that weighed the most heavily in his recovery.) The experts defined receptivity in terms of a consuming hangover, a period of contriteness and remorse. But Sean's hangovers either left him consumed with sensuality or made him sealed off, remote and on guard rather than contrite and remorseful, so I had given up trying in hungover circumstances. Now he was sober and in a loving, receptive mood.

As casually as I could, lest he think I was impugning his character, I said it might also be a good time to look into joining AA so that we could get the new year off to a sober start. After a few seconds of silence he said angrily, "I'll never understand you," and abruptly pulled his arm from under me and stalked out of the room. These sudden, chameleon changes made it hard to be constructive, to get a purchase on the problem. He got drunk that evening and abysmally so on Christmas Day, but most of the time he seemed better.

As per schedule, he began investigating positions early in 1964. He had luncheon dates and meetings and took a few trips out of town, always announcing when he returned that he had to work in New York, but most of the time he was home. It was, in some ways, a pleasant arrangement, the first time we had had time together and alone without the interruptions of his work or the children, and we took walks in the park and went to midday movies and afternoon matinees and I made salads and omelets for his lunch (occasionally I had a glass of wine, but I never joined him in his martini) and usually we made love after lunch. Sometimes, lying in bed in the middle of the day, bathed by the bright winter sun that shone through the window, we laughed at the absurd luxury of our situation. But overall it was depressing. As the months passed he began to drink more heavily, getting puffy in the jowls and stomach and at times, even when perfectly cold sober, he was withdrawn, absent-mindedly putting his arm around me when I bent over to give him a cheery kiss.

As spring rolled around I tried very hard not to press him as to when he would return to work. Whenever I did he accused me of lack of faith and reminded me that at this stage of his career —he was thirty-nine—it was vital that he make the right connection. I desperately wanted to believe it would all work out, but his constant presence began to get on my nerves, especially on those days when he hung around the apartment just reading and drinking. I tried to fire his interests by suggesting he write articles on aspects of the law—he shrugged off the idea—and to distract myself I tried my hand at writing a children's story. It concerned the adventures of a field mouse (Nicholas had tried to make a pet of one in East Hampton) and for authenticity and to get out of the apartment I spent hours at the Museum of Natural History researching rodents, learning that field mice lived in tunnels burrowed under the earth. That's the way it seemed that we were living, underground, a secret life. Time was standing still, stagnating, and it worried me that the seepage would have an adverse effect on the children.

They were my jewels, and their well-being concerned me every bit as much as did Sean's. While trying not to belabor the point and frighten them, I had told them something about alcoholism, that it was a disease and that was why Daddy sometimes drank too much. But I wanted to protect them from further anxiety, to shield them from knowing too much of the vicissitudes of our life, and yet it was hard to know how much was sinking through. We were playing charades, pretending that Sean was working, and though I was fairly certain the older two boys were on to the game, I thought the younger two were unaware. And then one day nine-year-old Nicholas, who was trying to make a boat out of a walnut shell, using a toothpick for the mast, said, "I can't make it work."

"Don't quit," I answered encouragingly. "You've almost got it."

"Is it ever okay to quit, to give up?" he asked softly.

"Here, let me try," I said, groping for the right answer. "And no, never give up unless there's absolutely no other way."

Finally at the end of the year Sean's decision to wait and choose was justified, and in January 1965 he joined a shipping firm as general counsel with an annual salary of $33,000 a year. My alcoholism literature was right. Sympathy and understanding had paid off, and we were back on the happiness trail. He went off to work in his Chesterfield and Homburg and came home at night with his attaché case full of work, and he cut down on the martinis so he could go over briefs. We took the boys down to see his fine new office with a view of the Battery and the harbor, and he told them that one summer we would all go on a long voyage on one of his company's ships. Scarcely three months later one of his former colleagues at the U. S. Attorney's office brought him home in the afternoon, so drunk he could barely stand. He went off to work the next morning and didn't return until midnight, blotto again, and a week later he was home for good, to sleep away the days and drink away the nights.

~5~

May Day 1965

Hurray, hurray, the first of May.

It had been a terrible spring in every way. Trouble, I discovered, came in big bunches. Immediately after Sean was fired, twelve-year-old Sean was stabbed in the stomach by a gang of youths, attacked on a beautiful afternoon while he was skateboarding at the crowded Central Park boat pond. There were people everywhere, mothers and children, tourists, kids, and suddenly the gang appeared, surrounded him, and then they were gone. He was hospitalized for five days and he was wonderfully brave, but it was an agonizing experience and Sean made it worse. He was tight when he came to the hospital, hysterical with rage, and the doctor asked me to please take him home, assuring me that our son would be all right. (Young Sean later said that it was the first time he realized that his father was an alcoholic.)

And then Curtis was asked not to return to school the following fall. Curtis was the sensitive, high-scoring four-year-old the school had sought seven years ago, but the new headmaster found him a discipline problem and said he needed a more structured school. He had called me to his office (just me, not both parents, which was strange, because Sean had been on the board of trustees for five years, but I went alone because he was in no shape to come with me), and as I didn't know how much he knew about my husband's drinking, I felt too vulnerable, too embarrassed to argue that what Curtis needed was a more structured home life and that changing schools would only compound the problem. He was a very verbose man and it was hard to get a word in edgewise, so I sat and listened to this stranger's lecture on child psychology, remembering that it was wide-eyed Curtis, at age nine, who had stepped protectively in front of me when drunken Daddy threatened to push me out of the window, and it was Curtis who could never get to sleep at night, listening, waiting for all hell to break loose. (I later learned that Sean had made his own private visit to the headmaster and cut through the verbosity by threatening to punch him in the nose for dismissing Curtis; this only served to add another strike against his son.) Hell was becoming the nightly norm. I could get through the day just by hanging in, being a mother; it was the nights that were bad, trying to play at being a wife.

Seamus, our youngest, was now six. He was a very active child and bright. And very loving. One night before going to bed he had tucked his old teddy bear up against Sean, passed out on the living-room rug, saying, "Daddy looks sad. He can sleep with Teddy tonight."

Daddy was indeed sad, and so was Mommy. My day began at seven-fifteen when the alarm went off. Most mornings I'd open my eyes to find my husband standing by our bed, eyes at half mast, a foolish smile on his handsome face, his whole body redolent of gin. In his hand would be my cup of coffee. This had always been my morning treat and our time together, a little while alone before bounding into the day's activities. Now it simply marked the awful beginning of another awful day.

"My beautiful girl," he'd say, slowly sinking down on the bed beside me while I struggled to get the coffee before it sloshed on the covers. He'd lean over for a kiss, and I'd turn away to avoid the blistering waves of gin. If he weren't too far gone to care, this could make him very angry, and the children would awaken to hear Daddy calling Mommy a rotten wife and demanding to know why I didn't love him anymore. So I tried to be as nice as I could, lamely reassuring him that I loved him very much, though the sight of him made me sick and sad, too depressed to think, and I'd sip the coffee and wait for a chance to slip out of bed, trying to avoid a scene. This could be difficult, because he was almost six feet tall and very strong, and if he didn't want me to get up, there was little I could do, except to remind him that the children must not be late for school. This usually worked, for he still wanted to be a responsible parent.

If he didn't doze off he'd come and stand by the breakfast bar while they ate, sipping his gin and orange juice, his head slightly awobble, a benign, bleary-eyed buddha. Occasionally he asked the boys about school, but they weren't very responsive, appearing totally absorbed in reading the back of cereal boxes. I tried to act as if everything were normal because I knew it was difficult for the children; but I didn't know what to do about it, other than to try to keep the peace, to get through the day.

After the final push to find the missing shoe or book—now more of a chore than ever because Sean kept questioning me as to why I was so disorganized, following me about and getting in the way—we'd be ready for school at eight. In the past he had always taken them, but now the best he could manage was to stand with us at the elevator, unshaven and unsteady, the boys solemnly receiving his goodbye hug. They were careful never to look up at the other passengers.

But as soon as we got outside and on the way to school, they came alive, racing ahead to be with friends or chattering about the busy day ahead and what was to happen when school got out. The morning city usually made me feel more cheerful, too, and sometimes I'd set off on one of my long walks down Madison Avenue, killing time looking at shop windows full of art, ugly fruit, books, bathroom fixtures, lighting fixtures, toys, potted plants, shoes, dresses, furs, table settings, jewelry, something for everyone who could soothe the soul by spending money. Other times I'd be the A&P's first customer, adding time to my shopping by chatting with the manager, who always had lots to say on the subject of feeding and rearing his six children. He usually summed up his point of view with "takes a minute to make 'em, a lifetime to pay for 'em." After depositing the groceries at home, I'd set off at ten for the Society Library or the museum. Several mornings a week I went directly to church from school. The Mass would be ending, and I'd sit there for an hour, asking God to help Sean and to help me, and this usually made me feel more at peace and better able to cope with the bleakness of going home to the silent apartment where my alcoholic slept or sat, morose and zombie-like, at the dining-room table, sipping gin and studying, page by page, *The New York Times.* He had been drunk every day since he'd been fired, and he wouldn't talk to me, even answer my questions when I asked him if he wanted something to eat.

At three I picked the children up at school. Being boys, they needed to be run, and usually we went to Central Park and on bad days to the Metropolitan Museum or the Museum of Natural History. Now these outings were more important than ever, because it meant the boys could bring their pals along and have fun without worrying about Daddy; bringing them home could be embarrassing. When we returned to the apartment around five Sean was usually shaved and dressed, often in a business suit and not visibly tight. It was as if the rest of the day hadn't happened, and he greeted us with hugs and smiles the way he used to do when he came home from work.

After the boys were settled in he'd put on his hat and coat and go off for the evening paper, taking his attaché case along. It stood like the little tin soldier in the front hall closet, patiently waiting for the subway trip downtown. There were times when he wouldn't return until midnight, absolutely stoned, but more often he'd be back with the paper under his arm and the attaché case in his hand, just the way it used to be. Only now the case contained a quart of gin instead of briefs. And then, after carefully hanging up his coat, he'd ask me, courteously and affectionately, as he had for so many years, if I would like to have a martini. This was the best part of the day even though I knew it was make-believe.

The children ate their supper, and then, while the older boys did homework and the younger two bathed and played, we'd sit in our accustomed living-room chairs, he with the evening *Post* and me with the morning *Times*, discussing the ways of the world. It was as if nothing had gone awry. At forty-one he had a dynamic interest in everything, a point of view, buttressed now by fifteen years of working and endless hours of reading. He was an attractive, gray-haired man in his prime, and, grasping for the pieces of our former good life, I'd push the rest of the twenty-four hours out of my mind and pretend that all was the same.

But inevitably, by the end of the second martini, served in an Old Fashioned glass, iced but without the rocks, and no matter what the original topic—politics, books, the stock market—we were into our evening's round. It was my fault. During the day when I was numb with despair, all I could think about was trying to help Sean and trying to keep a decent life for the children; but at night the drinks brought other feelings to the surface. I was resentful, angry that he was making a mess of our life, and, fortified with the false courage of booze, I began to fight back. I'd question what sounded like a preposterous, intoxicated statement, reminding him that he never spoke that way when sober, or I'd let slip the fact that he was too bright to be sitting around drinking all day. Or, less soberly, more resentfully, I'd blurt out that if he were so smart, why wouldn't he see a psychiatrist or join AA.

He in return would mock me for suggesting he had a drinking problem, scoff at the suggestion of AA, and, by way of riposte, say I was obviously getting a little mental and, though he had little faith in them, perhaps I should see a psychiatrist. Round after round, well into the third martini, until I'd say, now adamantly aggressive, that if he didn't stop drinking I'd leave him, to which he would respond in a serious and sinister voice that if I ever tried I'd be dead. His eyes would narrow, the corners of his mouth turn down, and he'd jab his finger at me, saying in a quiet, bitter voice, "You're my wife. Don't ever forget that. My wife, dead or alive."

"Don't talk like an idiot," I scolded, trying to hide my fear by treating him like a child. There would be more accusations and threats. Finally, a slightly awash Mommy and now quite drunk Daddy (if he were still ambulatory) would put the children to bed.

To six-year-old Seamus's whispered "Will Daddy really kill you?" I'd say reassuringly, "Of course not, honey. He's just been drinking too much." I had briefed them on his illness, explaining that Daddy didn't mean to be mean, that he loved us all, but that he was a victim of alcoholism, and this made him drink too much and say things he didn't believe.

Sometime after nine I served dinner. After another drink it didn't bother me too much the way he ate, his face almost in his plate, food more often going on the floor than in his mouth. I had become inured and calmly ate, concentrating on the view from the dining-room windows. Almost every night I could see the back of a man in a window across the courtyard; he was painting, a canvas propped up on the easel before him, and I could never make out what the picture was and often wondered why he did it every night.

Immediately after dinner my alcoholic would stagger into the bedroom, turn on the television, and collapse on the bed. Television is a great boon for alcoholics, just as it is for other sick people. It takes minimal thought, no in-put, yet provides a sense of being involved. Sean was especially fond of watching football and skiing, his two favorite sports. However, any program was better than none. Even when he appeared to be sleeping and I'd turn it off, he'd immediately rouse himself and demand that it be reinstated; so every night I went to bed with the late movie going. By then I was tight enough to be oblivious to it. I knew I was drinking too much, but I didn't care; it was the only way I could lull myself to sleep.

But that wasn't the end of our perfect day. My alcoholic had had considerable rest during the preceding sixteen hours, and around one or two he'd be back up, usually for the night, often playing records. The cast album of *Camelot* and Bob Dylan's "Mr. Tambourine Man" were special favorites. Sometimes he'd barge back into the bedroom to take up the argument where we had left off earlier, and there was no way to stop the harangue other than noncommittally to let it run its course. Either way, I was awakened after a few hours from my own drugged sleep, and then I'd lie in bed, waiting for the night to pass, playing dead dog if he came back to bed. It helped when I could conjure up memories of the happier past, but more often my thoughts were dominated by the dismal present. Around five I went back to sleep again.

Sometimes Sean was sick in the middle of the night. I'd listen to him retching or having the dry heaves, and then he'd crawl shakily back to bed and lie there shivering. This usually made me feel desperately sorry for him (but not always, because I was also desperately tired of cleaning up the mess in the bathroom), and I'd stroke his forehead and tell him I loved him and that we had to do something to save ourselves. He would nod and say that he loved me more than anything, and for a few days thereafter he would try not to drink, or at least to drink very little, spending his days resting and reading, a nervous, withdrawn convalescent.

But it never lasted, and soon he'd be drinking again from dusk to dawn so that by seven-fifteen in the morning he was sufficiently stewed to blot out the rest of the day.

65

Sipping my lukewarm coffee, stroking my poor tired husband's head resting in my lap, I wondered where God had gone. Once it had all seemed so simple: work and love, as the man said, but my Phi Beta Kappa couldn't work because he couldn't stop drinking, and I couldn't seem to love him the right way. He was only getting worse.

In the back of my mind I thought about leaving him. But my literature said this was wrong. Over and over I read that I was the key to his recovery, that patience and understanding were not only essential but pivotal. One pamphlet (*The Alcoholic Husband —A Message to Wives*) first censured those who "took jobs and flaunted their earning capacity in the face of men who no longer seemed willing and able to work [or] barred their husbands from the threshold, or went back to their own families, taking the children with them. . . . Some of them arranged legal separations or sought freedom through the most drastic step of all, divorce." (This was published in 1954, and one can only hope that it is now out of print.)

And then it described the way to help: "Mostly, however, the wives of these problem drinkers who no longer drink seem to have clung desperately to the hope that somehow, some day, their husband would regain the qualities that had once made marriage seem such a promising venture. In spite of poverty, in spite of heavy emotional and physical burdens, these wives continued to seek knowledge and understanding that would provide a way out of their dilemma. They got it."

For a long time all I was to get out of such advice was a paralyzing sense of guilt. It was painful enough to love Sean and see him transformed, but this was made even more painful by the inference that I wasn't loving him the right way. I kept clinging to the hope that I could help, and I tried my best to be stoic, understanding, wise; but I was failing, failing him and failing the children, too, and this made me feel even more guilty. Guilty and trapped. But who was the spider and who was the fly?

The ship's clock on the mantel chimed eleven. Four more hours to kill before the children were out of school and how many more days and nights. "There has to be an answer," I whispered to myself as I stood gazing out of the window. And suddenly, out of the bright blue sky, a direct beam from the distant gleaming spire of the Chrysler Building, the answer came to me.

Sean was sick. Sick with the disease of alcoholism. And if I couldn't help him with the right attitude, then he needed treatment by someone who could help him. And that's what doctors were for. Sick people who needed treatment. The time had come to call a doctor.

Up until that moment it hadn't seemed a solution. I had read over and over that alcoholism was a "baffling disease" and that the symptoms were, as my *Primer* said, manifest "chiefly in the uncontrollable drinking of the victim," and the uncontrollable drinking led the victim to act quite predictably like a drunk— heedless, irresponsible, sometimes maniacally, even mean. I had tried again and again to get Sean to see a psychiatrist, but since he refused I didn't see what a medical doctor, an internist, could do for him. And I kept remembering my mother-in-law's scornful "cockroaches and all" doctor, and I was afraid, my literature notwithstanding, that this might still be the prevailing medical point of view.

Now, however, since he had been drunk daily for the past two months, from the day he was fired to the present, there were physical symptoms. He slept most of the day, almost as if he were in a coma, his stomach was heavily distended, and there was a network of thin red lines crisscrossing his skin. Any good doctor would certainly understand that, however baffling the cause, my husband was in a pathological state and needed treatment. I went to the desk telephone and dialed the only internist we knew, hoping he would have positive suggestions to make. I shall call this man Dr. Pierce.

He was a graduate of Columbia University's College of

Physicians and Surgeons, a man close to Sean's age, with a Park Avenue practice and an impeccable social as well as professional background. I didn't know him well, having spent most of my time with the obstetrician and pediatrician, and the two times I had consulted him he had referred me to specialists. Although I found him reserved and a bit off-putting, he was highly recommended by friends and, more importantly, he had treated my husband on several occasions. (The previous fall Sean had slipped in the tub while tight and painfully injured his neck. Suspecting a slipped disc, Dr. Pierce had referred him to three specialists, who variously recommended traction and bed rest at home, an operation, and prolonged hospital bed rest. Sean treated himself with pain killers and gin and recovered, independent of their advice.)

I identified myself to the nurse, who put me through.

"Yes," he said in his cold, formal voice, "this is Dr. Pierce."

I introduced myself again, giving my first name to establish a closer rapport. And then I began to lose confidence. "I don't know what to do," I began, faltering. "It's my husband. I'm afraid he's very sick—that is, he's drinking all the time, night and day, for the past two months. And there's no way to stop him."

"I'm sorry," he said firmly, decisively, "there's nothing I can do."

"But there must be something," I insisted, taken aback by his attitude. "You've seen him. He's in terrible shape. Can't you come and give him a shot or something to make him stop—at least long enough to sober him up?"

"Stop what?" he asked bluntly. "Is he hemorrhaging or hallucinating?"

"No . . . I don't think so. I don't know—but he can't go on like this, drinking himself into a coma day after day." I waited, feeling that I was ratting on Sean, telling the doctor something too personal for his pure clinical ears.

"I'm sorry," he reiterated in the same cool tone, "there's nothing I can do."

After a few seconds of silence I said goodbye. I was sorry I had called.

In the next five years I was to find that Dr. Pierce's attitude was, in essence, the prevailing one. He was the most aloof and disdainful of the doctors I consulted, but his medical opinion, if it can be so categorized, represented the consensus. It was as if the sickness, being caused by booze, had no validity. Sean didn't have to drink the stuff, and if he persisted, then there was no reason—and presumably no way—to treat him. And though he seemed to have a specialist for every ailment short of the common cold, Dr. Pierce didn't recommend that I consult a doctor or psychiatrist or anyone else more knowledgeable about alcoholism. (At the time I didn't know such doctors existed.) He simply dropped the problem and took no further responsibility for its consequences.

At the time, mired in my own hangups (the guilt and worry and shock and sadness) and in my ignorance (my literature only told me how to effect recovery, not how to deal with failure), I glumly accepted Dr. Pierce's implication that alcoholism was totally outside the realm of medicine. Perhaps he spoke as he did simply because he didn't know how to deal with a drinking problem, but at the time I called I had the definite impression that he didn't consider treatment his concern. That made me more depressed than ever and also more confused. Two years had passed since I started reading about alcoholism and learned that it was a disease, and yet this medical man didn't appear to give a damn. It was simply a matter of bad luck, a bad habit.

Or was it?

6

Causes and Cures

During this period when my husband's alcoholism was becoming glaringly evident but his sober days were clearly recalled, friends used to ask me two questions. The first one was: When did it begin?

The question was always asked sympathetically, coupled with the observation that he had been such a fine person, a good father, charming, bright, a man who had everything going for him. (Later the question never came up; he was accepted simply as an alcoholic, as if he had no previous life style.) It was a perfectly reasonable question, but I never knew how to answer it, and my alcoholism literature never helped.

Maybe it began in the womb and he was born with a special sensitivity to alcohol; but one pamphlet I read stated that "the individual who develops alcoholism is not a born alcoholic," though it later noted that "only people with the X-factor capacity to develop addiction to alcohol become alcoholics." (This *Alice in Wonderland* rationale probably referred to the enzyme imbalance theory or perhaps to hyperglycemia, an abnormal concentration of glucose in the blood, a condition now being investigated in relation to alcoholism.)

Or perhaps it began at age thirteen, the complex age of puberty, when his father died and as the eldest son he assumed his father's role, comforting his lonely, dependent and sometimes drunken mother, urging his younger siblings on to achieve academically and cope socially, zealously carrying out his grandfather's commission: "Bear in mind that your mother is depending on you to show the way to others." His sister, six years younger, told me that he literally held the family together, helping with homework, organizing chores, mediating disputes, serving as liaison with stingy Uncle George, all the while taking gentle care of his mother. If she passed out on the kitchen floor, he put a pillow under her head and a blanket over her, never criticizing, always praising, extolling her virtues as a mother, ever striving to be the perfect son and surrogate father to his brothers and sister. Yet losing his father and then contending with an alcoholic mother must have been painful and damaging, even though he would never admit it. (Sometimes, in his cups, Sean would dramatically announce that he was a marked man, just like his father.) But my alcoholism literature told me "the disease is not caused by social and emotional problems."

Or perhaps his alcoholism was related to World War II. Until he became sick, Sean never mentioned the war with deep bitterness and rarely spoke of actual fighting experiences. The only indication that war had left its mark was his unusual sensitivity to loud, sharp noises, such as backfires, extreme apprehension of anything that sounded like gunfire. But after he became chronically ill and was presumedly suffering with the d.t.'s, he constantly hallucinated, not about frisky pink elephants but about the German and Russian soldiers who were after him. I could never understand why, and then after he died I found this letter, written to his mother in May 1945. He had just been discharged from a hospital outside Paris, where he had spent three months recovering from wounds received while fighting in the Battle of the Bulge and was awaiting reassignment. He was twenty years old.

Paris, 5/45

Dearest Mother,

It's hard to believe I am no longer with the 84th Division. However, the 84th that I knew was completely destroyed last November in our first attack. Now that the censorship ban has been lifted I can give you some idea of the casualty rate. Listen well, because I will never speak of it again. I'm sick forever of being surrounded by misery, violence and tragedy. War is no process of cleansing, no sins are purged, men are not brought back to faith and humility. Instead, disbelief and cynicism take precedent.

It should be sufficient to say that I was one of the original men left in the company of 200, and one of three "Old Men" left in my platoon (forty men). We had run through about two hundred replacements in my platoon alone—of course, all of these were not killed, although too many of them were—the majority were wounded or trench foot cases, caused by wandering around in the snow or wallowing in mud for weeks at a time.

I haven't heard from my best friend in the company. I'm just keeping my fingers crossed, it's too late to pray —three of my other good friends from ASTP were killed. My very good friend, Corkill, the 30 year old Irishman, was killed. This is not a survey but maybe will help explain some of my letters written during combat life. I was really "off my top" two or three times, and I have acquired a categoric abhorrence for impartial violence. I'm driven by the thought that propelled Somerset Maugham's hero in *The Razor's Edge*—"the dead look so dead when they are dead." Rather morbid but very fundamental. When I read "light casualties," I think, my God, the tragedy that the loss of one man brings to one small corner of the globe.

What I desire more than anything else in the world right now is faith to replace hope. Not the faith of the Irish washerwoman but the faith of Descartes. Yet I know that without his genius, it will take a miracle. Thank God I realize that a life can be made happy without faith or even passing pleasure if love exists—love for life, love for a person, and even for people in general.

> Your loving son,
> Sean

Obviously combat life in the battle of Germany had been a searing experience, so much so that sometimes he had felt that he was "off his top," so much so that other than this letter he didn't talk about his abhorrence of violence until he was chronically sick and then it came out obliquely, a paranoia that he was being pursued by German and Russian soldiers and spies. However, my pamphlet on alcoholism continued to explain, "Nor is it caused by bad nerves or personality aberrations."

Conceivably it could have begun in 1956 when we bought our house in East Hampton. At the time we hadn't an inkling that the village was about to emerge as a crucible of calculated chic, a cauldron of competition for the right houses, the right friends, the right clubs, with the most points clearly scored by giving and going to the right parties. We bought our house because East Hampton was two hours closer to New York than Sean's home town in New England and because the location was simple and rural and beautiful.

But the simple life didn't last very long, and after a few

summers social life had accelerated to a dizzying pace. The flag went up as the train pulled in on Friday evening, with barely time for a quick drink and a fast swim before the first relentless round of cocktail parties, dinner parties and drinky Sunday luncheons, with the last shot fired over Sunday night's potable pain killers.

Our inn-keeping added further socializing. Although I did the actual inn-organization with the help of a maid and Sean functioned solely as the patron and groundskeeper as we would have done with or without the inn, we both felt compelled to show our warmth and hospitality by inviting guests for an occasional drink, either at lunch or before we set off on our evening rounds. It seemed essential at the time, but I'm not sure that's what made the inn a success. One of our guests, an older woman (most of our clientele were swingers, our age, friends or friends of friends), said she liked to come because "the minute you step inside you can tell it's a house full of love."

We joined the right club, and after a morning of tennis the right thing to do was to go to the pool for a swim and then order a drink from the handy bar, which always meant two, because who wants only one drink? Thus, Mondays meant a compounded hangover, best treated by several hairs of the dog that night, with Tuesdays through Thursdays the only time off for good behavior. And then Friday it was time to start partying again. It was as a friend said one day shortly after I began to realize that Sean had a problem. He asked how we were, and I said, "Not so hot. I'm afraid Sean's drinking too much."

"Oh?" he answered in a philosophic, almost debonair manner. "Well, aren't we all?"

However, I don't really think the East Hampton social circus was what caused it. Nor do I believe that his descent into alcoholism was caused by his not being made a partner in his law firm. This has often been posited by friends, and in terms of chronology that, in fact, was when the alcoholism began to emerge. Sean had carefully built up an image of himself as a Wall Street lawyer, the right law school, the right firm, even the right clubs. (In addition to the East Hampton club, he was a member of a downtown athletic club and an exclusive Wall Street lunch club.) It was an image that meant a great deal to him (far more than it did to me; he was the Williams fraternity man and I was the Bennington girl, the do-your-own-thing non-belonger), and not being made a partner was the first real chink in his armor. But just as not every veteran of World War II and not every East Hampton swinger became an alcoholic, I can't ascribe the cause to his not being made a partner. He was one of at least 80 percent who didn't make it, and those I knew went their sober ways elsewhere. (And conversely, I have since known one or two partners who became alcoholics.) It might have been the immediate trigger but not what caused it nor when it began. By then the psychological pattern was already established, and instead of remaining a heavy drinker he had already tripped over the line.

Alcoholism literature is full of the definitions of the beginning, middle and final stages of the disease, and this is of paramount importance, both as a warning of the consequences of progressive drinking and thus, hopefully, as preventive medicine —and also in so far as the inevitable pattern gives credibility to the concept of alcoholism as a disease. However, knowing the progressive pattern was of little, if any, help in knowing how to stem the tide. Not being a seer or a psychiatrist, I don't know when it began. The real point for me was: What to do about it?

I never once stopped loving Sean, but as long as he was as free as anyone else to go out and buy that first daily bottle, there was no way to reach out and help. His mind and spirit were too obfuscated by drink.

The second question that good friends used to ask wasn't really meant as a question. It was really meant as advice. This question was: Can't you get him to AA?

To the non-alcoholic it sounds like such a reasonable and simple solution. Hey, hey, take it away, AA. If I heard the question once, I heard it one hundred times, the same question, over and over, from friends, acquaintances and, on one occasion, from a business associate I didn't even know. He called me one day and in a no-nonsense voice demanded to know what I intended to do about my husband's drinking; and, with a strong edge of exasperation in his voice, he polished off his painstaking concern with the familiar and inevitable: Can't you get him to AA?

How, I asked patiently, did he propose I get him there?

Alcoholics Anonymous is an extraordinary organization, or fellowship, for which I have the highest regard and admiration. It has been the single most effective means of the victims learning to live with this "baffling disease." It was the first organization persuasively to present the alcoholic as a sick person, suffering from a definite disease. It was largely responsible for updating the Dark Age's concept of the drunk as bum, to be locked up in prison, or the insane asylum, or stashed in a rat-hole back room, or at best, when circumstances permitted, kept more tidily in his cups with a hired keeper. Whatever the economics of the scene, treatment usually consisted of trying to keep drunks out of sight and hence out of mind, and if the sot decided to sober up, it was largely a do-it-yourself proposition.

But today, almost forty years after AA was established, we live in an enlightened age. There are posters on subways and buses, flash cards on television, radio announcements, articles in the press, advertisements of AA meetings in newspapers, books by alcoholics turned AA, and an extensive number of pamphlets published by the National Council on Alcoholism and AA, all stressing the fact that alcoholism is a disease, that the alcoholic is a sick person, and that help is as close as the nearest AA meeting.

But the catch is that the alcoholic has to find his own way to the meeting. He has to want to try to live without alcohol. That means he wants to stop drinking, no mean task when by definition he lives to drink.

A Sensitive, Passionate Man

There was never a time when both Sean and I weren't completely aware of the existence of AA. We didn't live in a vacuum or a remote outpost of the world, and for a time joining seemed like the most reasonable and simple solution to me, too, and I brought it up many times, even volunteered to go with him on the assumption that the buddy system would make abstinence more palatable. But my timing was always off, the right moment of receptivity was too elusive, so I dropped the subject until he was fired the second time. Panicky, I decided to go directly to the source and ask for help in getting him to join.

I wanted him to go to a meeting where he'd find people with similar background with whom he could readily identify so he couldn't rationalize that they were different types with different problems. Several friends who had advised me to get him to AA had said that members would do anything to help each other, and I wanted him to become involved with a basically executive group, one in which there might conceivably be members who would help him to re-establish himself professionally.

I called an old friend, a vice-president of a large corporation. Cautioning me to use discretion (he was not AA and apparently considered membership to be a sub-rosa matter), he gave me the names of two men, one a stockbroker and the other an insurance man and each a member of an Upper East Side chapter.

Both men were very sympathetic, saying they knew how difficult it was for me and the family. But both also said there was nothing they could do until my husband truly wanted to join; soliciting his membership might well turn him off for good. In sum, although AA offers the most available, effective means of living with the disease, these men were really saying that treatment was still a do-it-yourself proposition.

AA is in every way an admirable organization, with some five hundred thousand members in the United States. But at best that's only 10 percent of the total five to ten million alcoholics in this country; nevertheless, it is considered to be the most viable solution to the problem. And yet where but in limbo does it leave the other 90 percent, the alcoholics who are either too sick to do it themselves or the ones who aren't turned on by the necessary operation bootstrap?

My literature told me that a basic tenet of AA membership is acknowledging "a Power greater than ourselves [to] restore us to sanity" and making a decision to "turn our will and our lives over to God as we understand Him." Faith healing is great if it works, but if I were an alcoholic, helplessly dependent on drink, physically ill and mentally confused, I might well find the mystique too amorphous a solution to my problem, just as I would if a doctor told me to go pray my way out of cancer or schizophrenia. And unfortunately I wasn't group-oriented, and I doubt that my resolve not to drink could be sustained by listening to other people confess and describe their sins and resurrections or by constantly repeating my own. For better or for worse, at heart I am not a penitent; and neither was Sean.

It was for similar reasons that I didn't go to the Al-Anon Family Group meetings. Al-Anon is an organization structured similarly to AA for husbands and wives of alcoholics (both those who have turned AA and those who have not) who come together to help each other gain the support and strength to help themselves (and thus, indirectly, to help their alcoholics) through an exchange of knowledge and experience. My literature told me that if nothing else, joining Al-Anon would make me feel "less alone," but I didn't see how. I felt alone because I couldn't communicate with, much less help, the man I loved, my own personal alcoholic.

I also rejected the recommendation that our children become involved in Al-Anon. What good would it do them to be pushed into a social relationship with other such orphans of the storm, total strangers with whom they shared but one thing in common—a drunken parent? It was their own relationship to their own father that mattered to them, and I had explained as often, as compassionately and as intelligently as I could that he was sick, not deliberately heedless or irresponsible, not because I thought they could really understand but because I didn't want them to give up loving him. He was an alcoholic, yes, but more than that he was their father. (I had also told them that there were more than five million other alcoholics, but for them, as for me, there was little comfort in this googolplex factor.) Since I could not at this point see my way, psychologically, to leaving Sean (drunk or sober, I loved him and wanted to help and protect him), it seemed far better that they make friends by choice, not by stigmata. I wanted to bring the normal, the healthy into their lives, not perpetuate the sickness by having them mingle with children of the sick.

In retrospect, and especially in the light of today's acceptance of all manner of group therapy (it was just then beginning and was treated in the media as an almost obscene joke), I think I was wrong not to have at least tried Al-Anon, just as I was wrong not to pursue every single available means of trying to help Sean, no matter how redundant, inconclusive or dead-end it sounded. Yet, having lived with a thinking man, I found simple solutions to complex problems somewhat inane. Or perhaps it was simply that at heart I'm not a joiner and wouldn't have been one were I an alcoholic.

It seemed to me that the only real kind of help for Sean was psychiatric. For the first thirty-eight years of his life he had done everything right, and then, inexplicably, he had lost control and couldn't stay away from the bottle; yet, the only reward was the dubious pleasure of watching all his past efforts go down the drain. My alcoholism literature said that "alcoholism is a baffling disease, with no known cause and no known cure," but that wasn't good enough for the man I loved. There had to be a reason for the sudden, swift addiction, and I felt a good psychiatrist could plumb the depths and possibly come up with the right answer.

But whenever I suggested this to Sean he turned a deaf ear, saying he had neither a psychiatric problem nor a drinking problem and it was all in my mind.

So AA couldn't take it away because Sean wouldn't go to a meeting, and even though my literature said that alcoholics were sick, the doctor refused to treat the patient, all of which left me locked into a never-never land, bounded on one side by the hand-wringing, guilt-engendering proposition that alcoholism is a disease and on the other by the indifferent once-a-drunk syndrome. But I loved him too much to give up, and there was still one theoretic remedy left.

My literature indicated that in many instances the recognition of the need to join AA was contingent on a concept known as "hitting the bottom." This was a murky, relative area. For some it was the loss of a job (my alcoholic had already lost two); for others, a bad accident (a *Times* article told of a woman who had joined AA after falling into her elegant coffee table and breaking her collarbone; my alcoholic's recent fall in the tub hadn't done that for him). But for many more, the bottom had to be more jolting—poverty, jail, mental institutions, loss of family, etc.

In substance, "hitting the bottom" meant enduring painful, degrading, sometimes gruesome experiences which, at some indeterminate point, and assuming the alcoholic survived, would lead to recovery, most generally defined as membership in AA.

I could dimly see the handwriting on the wall, and the future looked bleak, even frightening. (One night I dreamed I was walking along a New York street, physically transformed into a fragile Ann Harding-looking figure, wrapped in a bright-green coat and wearing immaculate white kid gloves, and I saw Sean transformed into a bum, lying asleep in a tenement doorway.) But loving him, I saw no choice but to adopt the Hang on, Sloopy posture recommended and, with as much faith and forebearance as I could muster, ride it out with him until he "hit the bottom" and finally joined AA.

I didn't really know what I was getting into, but even so it struck me as the most negative rehabilitation program known to modern medicine.

The Lonely Life
Summer 1965

Socially we were more or less on the shelf, and Sean, who had recovered from his prolonged spring bat and, though still drinking heavily, wasn't always drunk, was aware of the increasing ostracism. It had an insidious way of creeping into our good days, days when he was sober and we all joined together to relive a happy family life. I recall one sparkling Sunday beach day when we all went for a swim in the ocean and then set off together for a walk, only to see a group of our best friends and their children gathered together for a picnic with the works: steamers, corn, tomatoes, hot dogs, hamburgers, wine, and soda pop for the kids. We had always been an integral part of these family picnics, which were always held on "our beach" because our house was the closest to the ocean and was a convenient base of operations, a place to go back for the forgotten ketchup, extra ice, the bathroom, etc.

The older boys tried to look away, as if they didn't see our friends, but Seamus, aged six and never at a loss for words, spoke up immediately.

"Why weren't we invited?" he demanded.

There were other beaches where they could have picnicked, and coming to ours, knowing we would probably appear, seemed a deliberate slight. I was at a loss and didn't know how to answer Seamus, but Sean did.

"I'm afraid it's because they think Daddy drinks too much," he said, smiling a little ruefully. It was the first admission of any kind I had heard him make, and for a second I saw a flicker of light at the end of the tunnel. But he second-guessed me and said, "None of your little lectures, please." We waved, self-consciously, and kept to ourselves, now walking along in awkward silence.

Alcoholism has been called the "lonely disease," and that it certainly is, not only for the alcoholic who gets locked into his own ossified world but also for his family. In the most basic sense, one is lonely because the alcoholic no longer functions as a father and husband and, in a broader sense, because the lonely disease infects normal social intercourse. In the most simplistic terms, and ignoring all other possible reactions, drunks are bores. Stray thoughts, nonsequiturs, diatribes, private jokes, garbled speech do not make conversation, and in time even one's closest friends and relatives shun association. And as boring (or depressing or irritating) as these sessions may be for friends, they are worse for a wife, painfully awkward, so that the most comfortable solution is to stay away from the social scene altogether. (The other solution is to join in, drink for drink, until awareness of the problem goes away.) In time I came to spot alcoholics at parties by observing their wives, the Mrs. Uptights, who, whether hovering anxiously by their husbands' side or clinging desperately to the opposite side of the room, were visibly braced for the moment when their mates would do or say something absurd, obscene, outrageous, or inane.

Theoretically the best solution is to establish a separate social life, but this isn't easy, especially for a non-working wife. Granted that a husband of an alcoholic wife may find it difficult to concentrate on his work because of worrying that the house may be burning down or the children running wild, he still has the day-time hours off and, in the evening, freer access to outside companionship. (If nothing else, he can always go to a bar for casual conversation and a change of scene.) But unless she has the money to buy social mobility—lunching out, taking classes, playing bridge, covering her absence with a hired sitter or cleaning woman—an alcoholic's wife is inevitably more house-bound, not only because of the time-consuming details of housework and child rearing but also simply because her own home—and not someone else's—is her natural habitat.

In the city I could get away while the children were in school and find diversion by going to a museum or the movies or just walking around town; and in the big, anonymous city I was less visibly alone and thus felt less isolated. It was different in the country. Other than the library, the local cultural center, a few shops on Main Street, there was no place to go within the immediate area other than the beach or the club, both of which were family-oriented; and going to either place with a drunken husband meant we automatically were rimmed off, as we had been that day at the beach, a separate unit encircled by an invisible but omnipresent perimeter of booze. And in the country it was difficult to go anywhere without my alcoholic because we lived in a rather remote area that necessitated transportation by car, and he was forever hiding the car keys (and the duplicates I had made) to prevent me from driving off alone. Being gregarious by nature, he refused to submit to the lonely life, even if it meant dogging my heels, and if I walked to the beach, he usually followed. So I stayed home much of the time or walked far up the beach where neither Sean nor anyone else could see me. But I missed companionship.

Sometimes, when my alcoholic was passed out, I tried to sneak off for drinks at cocktail time. My main reason for wanting to duck out was to get a more cheerful change of scene, a respite from his constant alcoholic presence. With our best friends there was a tacit understanding that if I could get away alone, fine, but otherwise no. However, this seldom worked out comfortably, because my husband had an almost uncanny sense of my presence and usually tracked me down, either by bike or cab; or he wiped out the pleasure of my escape by raising hell when I returned. In essence, the country house we loved and had bought as a refuge from the strictures of city living had become, more than the apartment, a trap, our own private little prison. I thought about breaking out but with no real intention of doing so. I was psychologically locked in, convinced I should stand by Sean.

In either locale it was uncomfortable for friends to stop by. An alcoholic in residence spins a web of gloom about a house, and a casual visit becomes a very self-conscious chore. If my alcoholic was sleeping, voices were hushed in the hopes of not awakening him; if he was relatively sober, conversation had to skirt the usual matters of work and play in which he no longer participated; and if he was drunk, there was no way to maintain continuity and interest.

On several occasions during the summer Sean took the social scene in his own hands and invited guests whom I didn't know and who didn't know what they were in for. Once it was a stockbroker, a man with three syllables to each of his three names, who arrived unexpectedly late one Friday afternoon with tennis racket in hand and dinner jacket over his arm.

During dinner the first night his host picked up his plate and threw it, food and all, through a window (I have forgotten why; perhaps to illustrate a forward pass), causing all nine syllables to say, quietly and correctly, that this was no way for a gentleman to act, especially in his own home. Other than the fact that I cut my foot on the broken glass the next morning (I had forgotten the incident—also, breakage was becoming quite commonplace —and was walking around barefoot) the weekend held few surprises, for our guest turned out to be a very serious tippler himself and readily adjusted to the scene by staying quietly and inoffensively drunk.

Another time it was a vice-president of a New York bank who arrived with his wife, Helen, in their cream-colored Cadillac, he in his yellow slacks and navy, club-crested blazer and she in her Pucci-type shirt and white slacks, hair freshly baked in the dryer. The first night went well enough in a high-spirited way, with cocktails, dinner and a few more drinks and then, at Sean's insistence, a midnight ocean swim, with George manfully joining in and Helen begging off because of her hair; and then more drinks and record playing until four.

The next morning at ten my alcoholic was still in a party mood, turning on the record player at full blast to awaken his guests, who got up, bleary-eyed but still smiling. Being ardent golfers, they set off with Sean for the club. At four in the afternoon they returned, my husband quite stoned, and George announcing with all the false cheer he could muster, "I think our friend here had a few too many at lunch." Sean immediately went to bed, and when I suggested to our guests that a little nap might refresh them, George obliged, but Helen insisted that she wanted to keep me company, presumably because she thought it was the nice thing to do.

Since I didn't play golf or garden (her two passions) nor share her deep affection for suburban life (she hated the city) and as she didn't have children, conversation was labored. She was one of those women who smile all the time, as if constantly pleased with whatever, including the pauses when neither of us could think of what to say next. This was making me nervous, so by way of refueling the conversation I suggested at five-thirty that we have a drink, my first of the day. She radiated agreement, and by seven, when Sean and George reappeared, she was a bit tiddly. Dinner kept being delayed, as Sean insisted that he and George had barely started on their first, then second, then third drink, and finally Helen gave up and tottered off to bed. George lasted through dinner, still manfully trying to join in the fun even though Sean was again on the verge of passing out and seemed

87

momentarily ready to topple from his chair, and then, pleading old age, George too went to bed.

When I got up the next morning they had already gone, leaving a game and hearty little note, thanking us for the wonderful weekend. I was glad they were gone. Unless they were close friends, terribly close, guests didn't make living with my alcoholic any less lonely, only more of a strain.

The most satisfying relief from the whole dismal scene was playing tennis. Sometimes it seemed that hitting that little white ball was the only reality, the only fact or feat that made any sense. If nothing else, it was an active process, and the only time I felt less than immobilized was time spent as my own agent on the courts. As soon as I approached our house I felt stifled, enervated. I told myself and the children over and over that Daddy didn't love us any less or mean to be difficult and that he needed understanding and love. But I was beginning to ask myself how long.

I had thought of a separation before, but only vaguely, hoping that by hanging in the miracle would happen, finding distraction for myself in the city and for the children in their schools. These distractions didn't exist in the country, and as the summer crept by a legal separation began to loom as the only sensible alternative.

If Sean was too sick to heal himself and if there was nothing doctors could do or would do to help him, what was the point in staying by his side when he was drinking progressively more and yet the bottom seemed nowhere in sight? We were being keelhauled in the wake of his alcoholism, and a separation would give us—all of us, Sean included—a chance to surface. I could be a better mother, the boys wouldn't be subjected to the crippling presence of a drunken daddy, and conceivably, without the constant pressures of a wife and children, Sean would be better able to get his bearings. I didn't need a book to tell me that alcoholics are guilt-ridden; I only had to remember what a wonderful husband and father he used to be to appreciate how he must feel now. And despite my good intentions, I couldn't maintain the right attitude. I was too emotionally involved, not just with him but with the children. Perhaps another woman, someone who wasn't mired in my conflicts, could better help him see the light and lead him out of the labyrinth. And I knew in my heart that were I his sister or client, Sean would, in these circumstances, recommend a separation—that is, if he were sober.

The possessiveness that made me a bit wary early on had turned obsessive, and he clung with demonic tenacity to what remained of his better days, often saying, "You're my wife and don't forget it. . . . You made a contract, a marriage contract, remember that, and I won't let you break it, ever." I knew he meant what he said, and even though he was now a drunk lawyer, and thus not a reasonable one, he was still shrewd, canny, and skilled in the law, especially as it affected his own interests.

I had never been a client, but I was surrounded by lawyers and had a built-in respect for the legal profession. My father, my sister's husband, my husband's youngest brother were lawyers, many of our friends were lawyers; all were first-rate men, and I had confidence in their ability to solve complex problems by judiciously advising the client and then diligently seeking a remedy. I knew there was another breed of lawyers, but I had never met any of them, and Sean had always said one should never mess around with second-raters and go to only the best firms for counsel.

However, when it came to seeking my own counsel I was in a quandary. I didn't want to go to one of Sean's friends and expose him to criticism on either a personal or professional basis. I asked the lawyer husband of a friend to recommend someone I didn't know socially, and the man he sent me to immediately reinforced my confidence in the legal establishment.

Mr. Edwards was a distinguished, somber man, seated behind a large mahogany desk in a dignified, wood-paneled office, and he listened with grave concern as I nervously, guiltily, often on the verge of tears, told him my troubles. He seemed almost like a father, and I waited, dejectedly but trustingly, to hear how he would solve my problems. With a deep sigh he began to speak.

He told me that he had worked with my husband on various Bar Association committees and that he had the highest respect for him, personally and professionally. (I wasn't really surprised they'd met, the lawyers' establishment being a kind of club.) He went on to say that the alcoholic problem was a tragic one and, unfortunately, all too familiar in the legal profession. However, since he had known my husband, he was reluctant to take my case, and the next thing I knew we were in a cab and on our way to the wrong side of the Wall Street legal tracks, arriving at a relatively run-down building, where we rode in a somewhat dirty elevator up to what was, unmistakably, a divorce mill, phony driftwood lamps and all. Being so summarily palmed off, as if I were doing something distasteful in terms of the establishment's fraternity, made me feel even more guilty; but I was too woebegone, too bewildered, to object.

I was introduced to Bert, the senior partner, defined as a friend of various important lawyers, and the wife of a very brilliant one who had now tragically taken to drink. We all looked sadly at each other, and then Lawyer Number One left and Lawyer Number Two took over. Bert did so in the following fashion: Taking my arm, he led me down the hall to a small office and introduced me to Ralph, his newly hired partner and former associate of Mr. Edwards. Ralph, he explained, was a crackerjack at cases such as mine and I would be in good hands—the best—and he himself would certainly be available if any problems arose.

I started my story again and Ralph listened raptly, as if I were telling tales of Jack the Ripper. By way of describing the difficulties my husband's drinking imposed, I mentioned that he had become violent on occasion and recently had punched a hole in the living-room wall. Ralph's face lit up as he said, "Get a Polaroid. We'll get a Polaroid picture of it. That's the first thing. Know how to use a Polaroid?"

"What good will a picture do? It isn't a big hole, just the size of his fist, and he could easily say the children did it with a baseball. Isn't it just my word against his?" I asked quietly.

Ralph smirked knowingly and pulled a portable electric heating coil out of his desk drawer and jammed it into a glass of water on his desk. "My finger's infected," he explained. "Doc says I have to soak it. You don't mind?" With that he plunged his thumb into the glass. It toppled, and the water streamed over the pile of papers on his desk. "We're going to prove this guy's a bastard," he continued, oblivious to the flood. "Now, did he ever beat you?"

I had begun to feel less like a sore-pressed supplicant and more like an impartial observer of what struck me as an absurd legal scene. I looked at this decidedly second-rater and made up my mind not to tell him of further tribulations. Why denigrate either Sean or myself?

"He isn't a bastard; he's an alcoholic," I answered, "and your papers are getting all wet."

"Oh." He laughed self-consciously. "That doesn't matter."

"Well, it matters to me," I said, rising. I left Ralph and went back to the senior partner's office.

The incident had caused some adrenaline to rise, and I told Bert that Ralph was in no way competent to deal with my husband, who, whatever his drinking problems, was a skillful lawyer with a very strong track record as a litigator and that if he didn't recognize this fact I'd have to tell Mr. Edwards and take my business elsewhere. Bert assured me that henceforth he would personally handle my case.

I began my story again. It was getting easier with each telling, and now my main concern was to make sure that he understood not just the facts of the case but that my husband had repeatedly said he would prevent any legal action and that, drunk

91

or sober, I was quite confident he would make every effort to do so. But Bert shrugged this off, saying I had a very good case, and he would immediately file the necessary papers so that I would have the apartment in my possession when it was time for the children to return to school in six weeks.

I also emphasized that my husband had said repeatedly that if I ever tried to leave him he'd kill me and that I had read too many newspaper accounts of "berserk husband slays wife and children" and that in no circumstances did I want to be around when Sean received word of the proceedings. At the time I had not read the following authentication of my fears:

> Generally speaking, all abnormal drinkers sooner or later show signs of paranoid nature—suspicion, jealousy, and ideas of persecution. Sometimes they are so dynamic that they eventuate in murder.
>
> (Edward Streker, M.D., *One Man's Meat*, Macmillan, 1953)

Neither had Bert, apparently. He blandly remarked, "They all say that and we haven't lost any wives yet." I mumbled that I didn't want to be his first casualty, and he said that the solution, then, was for me and the children to go away for the "cooling-off" period, a mere week or so, in which time my husband would be notified of my action and, after his initial anger had subsided, would see no recourse but to comply.

"After all," Bert said confidently, "he's a lawyer. He won't want to do anything to further jeopardize his reputation at the bar."

This struck me as a naïve assumption. I said nothing, as otherwise my new lawyer seemed to know what he was about. I went back to East Hampton to prepare for my getaway.

For the first time in my life I was going to run away, to go into hiding, and though I was determined to see it through, programming the move made me feel slightly like a criminal—

secretive, wary, lonely, and, most of all, terribly sneaky. Bert had asked for a picture of Sean so that he could be identified by the process server. Feeling like Judas, I sent off a Bachrach portrait, a study of a successful lawyer, lean, intelligent face, eyes looking steadily into the camera, a slight smile, a broad-shouldered, immaculate, well-tailored man, a person one could trust. Bert had also asked for a list of my husband's insurance policies, bank accounts, securities, the financial facts of our life that I had hitherto ignored, and I clandestinely rifled Sean's files, which was difficult, because he rarely left the house and would suddenly and silently appear when I thought he was safely passed out.

I had an uncashed check for $67, dividends on stocks Sean had given me, and to supplement this I began to sneak $5 and $10 bills whenever he gave me a $50 check for groceries. I had extra keys made for the car and hid these, along with a small cache of clothes, under one of the beds in a guest room. I told no one, and most certainly not the children, of my plans. I was afraid of what might happen if Sean found out.

On departure day I took the children to the club and told them that as a special treat they could charge lunch but that in no circumstances were they to leave or to lose their sneakers. Then I went home and waited for Sean to pass out so that I could safely remove our clothes and a few odd treasures, among them our photograph albums. These were a record of our courtship and the happy days of our marriage when the only real problems were finding baby-sitters and coping with the maneuvers of alternate-side-of-the-street parking. If I left these, I was afraid Sean would tear them up or never give them back to me.

By three in the afternoon he had passed out on the living-room couch, a bottle of gin on the floor beside him, and I tiptoed through the house, taking the things I needed. And then I left, sick at heart at the rotten state of our once honest, beautiful marriage.

Seamus, six, demanded to know why when I told the boys

to come quickly and get into the car, but the older ones, who were now nine, eleven and thirteen, sensed I was nervous and propelled him out to the club parking lot. I told them I would explain what was happening after we had gone twenty miles, and they rode along in silence while I concentrated on our getaway, certain that by now Sean would have found out what I was up to and sent the police in pursuit. As he said, it was his car, registered in his name, and I didn't put it past him to say I had stolen it.

When twenty miles were behind us I explained that we were leaving Daddy for a while because of his drinking and would take a short vacation before returning to New York for school, perhaps visit Daddy's sister and her children and maybe his brother and their Boston cousins. There were a few seconds of silence, and then Sean, the oldest boy, said soberly, "I'm glad we're doing this, Mom. It was getting to be too much."

Too much. Too much embarrassment and shame, too much confusion. How could they possibly understand what I had asked them to understand—that their father was sick, that he couldn't help the drinking, that he loved them as much as ever? For the first twelve years of his life young Sean had idolized his father, the man who could play football better than any of his friends' fathers, the man who had taught him to ski, who had helped him with homework and told him about honor and justice, the man who was now sitting around the pool drunk or passed out when his friends came over. All any of the four boys could do was to try to ignore what was happening, but at their ages it was impossible for them to understand. Driving along, I felt less deceitful. Now that we had left, life would be, at least, less embarrassing for them. I said we'd stop at a Howard Johnson's for dinner, and they perked up and the getaway seemed more of a lark.

But in the end we didn't leave. When my alcoholic realized we were gone, he sobered up, went back to the city, had the locks changed so I couldn't get in, put in an answering service to screen calls, and laid low. I had gone to stay with Sean's sister and then with his brother because I knew they were sympathetic and it would be less obvious than going to stay with my sister, and with only $150 of my own I couldn't afford to pay rent and had no place else to go. But after three weeks of camping on relatives we were all restless and weary of being the homeless in-laws, and I knew, no matter how cordially we were received, that an additional five persons in a household was an imposition. I was about out of money, and though my own family as well as my husband's was cheering me on, no one volunteered further financing and I was too proud to ask for it. This was my first taste of being a poor relation, and I didn't like it.

I kept calling Bert, who finally said the process was going to take longer than anticipated and suggested I rent a house in Connecticut, near to my sister-in-law's and close to New York, and enroll the children in school there until matters were straightened out. Without money of my own, this was impossible, and the children hated the mere suggestion of the idea. They wanted to return to New York, to their friends and, except for Curtis, to their familiar school. (Curtis had been accepted at a first-rate boys' school, the headmaster saying that though my son's grades were inconclusive, he was one of the most honest boys he had ever met.) I felt I owed them at least that much security, school being one of the few continuums left in their lives.

Then the miracle happened. The day before school was to open a doctor friend called to say that my husband had promised her that if I would return, he would stop drinking and see a certain psychiatrist noted for her success in treating alcoholics. Hopeful that Sean had "hit the bottom" and not knowing what else to do *vis-à-vis* the children, we piled in the car and headed back to our apartment in the city. Sean welcomed us back with open arms and tears in his eyes; he was a little tight, but I accepted that in terms of the strain he had been under.

We went to see the psychiatrist together. We were both very serious and Sean extremely nervous, as if he were frightened. She talked to him alone and then to the two of us, saying I had done the right thing in leaving and a brave thing in coming back but that if he didn't stay sober, then it was not my duty to stay with him, that, in fact, it would be better for myself and especially for the children to leave him.

She told us that Sean was seriously ill and definitely needed help to recover and said that though AA was excellent, it wasn't for everyone, and recommended that he see her twice a week, for a time as a private patient and later in group therapy. My husband nodded agreement and made an appointment for three days hence.

It was a lovely Indian-summer afternoon, and we held hands as we walked home. Sean was very grave, and I knew he felt alone and depressed, but for the first time in a long time I felt very confident and sure of him. Now that he had finally faced the problem, I believed he could cope with it. He had once been a heavy smoker, and seven years before he had quit cold one day. That was more than I could do.

On the day of his second appointment he left early, saying he wanted to walk. He didn't return until late that evening, sullen and plastered, and though I later pleaded with him to give it one more try, he never went back and the daily bottle of gin returned. When I called the psychiatrist she told me that apparently he wasn't ready yet. The self-help catch again.

8

Working for a New Life
Fall 1965–1966

Hope flared anew that fall when Bill, a former Williams classmate and also a Phi Bete, appeared on the scene and announced that he would finance law offices for Sean if the latter would handle all legal matters for an investment company he was going to establish. Bill was perfectly aware of the drinking problem; in fact, he had one himself (and, moreover, had recently divorced his alcoholic wife to the tune of $25,000 in legal fees, he told us with a certain amount of pride). But since he had, despite the drinking, managed a successful career in marketing and, through his shrewd investing, managed to increase his own inherited wealth, he saw no reason, he said, why a man as brilliant and capable as Sean could not produce, provided the work was sufficiently challenging.

They consummated the deal by getting royally drunk, after which proceeded, with Bill's money, to rent prestigious office space in which they installed elegant furnishings, and by the first of the year, 1966, they were ready to roll. Various business deals were immediately initiated, and in addition Sean was retained by several other clients. It was a beautiful idea, a generous gesture on the part of Bill, and the two of them were extremely pleased with the set-up, so pleased that they spent a considerable amount of time over martini lunches and afternoon cocktails at their respective clubs. They also kept a private stock in their respective offices, so that the only real difference in Sean's drinking pattern was that, during the daytime hours, he had a different setting, his office rather than his home. Even though I knew the alliance would *ipso facto* eventually end in disaster—no one, not even a drunk, wants a drunk for a lawyer—there was one decided plus in the arrangement. Because Sean was doing his daytime drinking elsewhere, I was freed of his oppressive alcoholic presence on a twenty-four-hour basis, and this gave me the time and energy to program the future. My faith in the wisdom of riding it out to the bottom was now pretty well shattered, as the trip was having a dismal effect on the whole family.

My literature had said "in spite of poverty, in spite of heavy emotional and physical burdens," I should stick by my husband, cling desperately to the hope that "somehow, some day [he] would regain the qualities that had once made [our] marriage seem such a promising venture." I was beginning to suspect that this was largely a euphemistic way of saying, "If your alcoholic can't work, go on relief; if the physical burdens include a broken jaw, turn the other cheek; and if the emotional burdens result in delinquent children or potential members of the next alcoholic generation, so what? In five or ten years Dad may come to realize he has a problem, join AA and sober up, a phoenix renewed—but on the ashes of his family's devastation." (Perhaps the most disturbing statement I read in my search for an answer was the "40 percent of alcoholics are children of alcoholics" and, later, "50 percent of drug addicts had at least one alcoholic parent.")

The bad times were taking their toll. Seamus, who had gotten off to such a promising start in nursery school at age three, was now having serious reading problems at age seven, and Curtis, the twelve-year-old who had been a leader and good student until the onset of his father's alcoholism, was now doing abysmally at his new school and had become very secretive and withdrawn. (He hated the school, considered one of the best in the city, and later told me that he and "a fat kid who always had ten bucks in his pocket" frequently skipped out, took a taxi to Chinatown for lunch, and then walked around the Bowery. "I kept thinking maybe I'd see Dad down there," he said.) Although the other two appeared to be going along as before at school, Nicholas, aged ten, was unnaturally quiet at home, as if his constant silence would make him invisible, and young Sean, always a very resolute boy, had become very tense at age fourteen.

As for me, though I still loved my husband and continued to be numbly heartbroken at the condition he was in, I was beginning to loathe my alcoholic. I could manage a cheery front as long as he wasn't around, but the minute he stepped into the room my spirits sank and my back went up. He was a terrible problem to live with, and my nerves were becoming raw. In addition to his abrasive alcoholic behavior, there were little things, like putting the chain on the door and then passing out so no one could get in. (Curtis learned to slip the chain loose with a dime, but when he wasn't around I was left to pound on the door and lean on the buzzer, often to no avail.) And he was always losing things—his hat or coat—and then nagging me as to what he had done with them. One night I blurted out that he wasn't acting like a man, and he knocked me down. My head hit the doorjamb and was bleeding. Furious, and convinced that my literature was garbage, I called the police. They came, and it was a real tenement scene, sobbing children clinging to weeping mother. Sean was so aghast that he appeared to sober up immediately, assuring the officers that it was only a little domestic squabble. I too was aghast at what he had done and at what I had done —and most of all, at what we were doing to our children—and when the police asked if I wanted to accompany them and my husband to the station house to press charges I shook my head, ashamed that I had let the situation get out of control. The officers left, but instead of saying he was sorry, Sean called me a bitch and charged off to the bedroom, Curtis following, crying, and saying over and over, "Please, Daddy, please stop drinking."

The next day I felt guilty, but I couldn't say I was sorry, because he would not apologize for hurting me and, more importantly, because he wouldn't even acknowledge Curtis's pleas, shutting him up by closing the bedroom door. I was getting tougher, tough enough to stand fighting with my husband on our own adult terms, but I couldn't stand to see him hurt the children. I was a mother as well as a wife and not a combination saint/martyr/male nurse/psychiatrist, and I was beginning to wonder whether my alcoholic was totally unlike all others or whether the authors of the sympathy-and-understanding doctrine used a vacuum for a frame of reference. The cut on my head healed but not the memory of the police and the children crying. I had to act to save them.

The drink shrink had said, flat out, that I had no duty to stay with my husband if he continued to drink. That was a vastly different point of view from the one in my literature, and I was rapidly coming to the conclusion that she was right and it was wrong. But there was one major stumbling block to following her advice: money.

The key to our rehabilitation, not my alcoholic's—AA meetings were free—was money, *my* money. I didn't really know how Sean was managing to pay the bills or how many securities he had left. These were locked away in his safety-deposit box along with the $8,000 in stocks he had given me. But I did know that to get at his money legally would take time. He was a lawyer and would be able to anticipate, delay and circumvent action endlessly, without any expense to himself and without being intimidated by the legal process. Or he could simply skip off to

Europe, taking his securities with him. Either way, the children and I would have to make do on thin air. I couldn't count on any meaningful support from relatives. My father was retired and lived on his pension, and my three brothers-in-law, although successful, each had large families to support.

I decided that the best plan was to keep the peace, such as it was, so that the children could continue as before while I put my energies into literally working my way out of this nightmare. That meant finding a job that paid well enough to cover the expenses of a housekeeper, lunches, etc., with a meaningful amount left over to establish a nest egg—no small task, as I was thirty-nine years old and hadn't worked in ten years. I had no acceptable office skills and no special training other than outdated experience in hotel and fashion promotion, a job market traditionally glutted with clever young women. (After we were married I had left the Plaza and occasionally worked on fashion publicity assignments until our third son was born.)

That fall I began poring over *The New York Times* classified section, where I learned that copywriters made the most money, and after working up a home-made portfolio of advertising campaigns I tried to pass myself off as one. Even with connections I deservedly got nowhere. However, the economy was good, and through friends I had an interview with an executive of a large public-relations firm who, much to my surprise, hired me to do a special two-week fashion promotion for a fee of five hundred dollars. To compensate for my lack of experience, I worked day and night on the assignment, sometimes taking a short nap after the children were in bed and then writing and rewriting my press kit until two or three in the morning. (Sean cooperated to the extent of going to bed, instead of staying up and playing records, when I worked.) In the end, the client and all concerned were pleased. I immediately received another assignment, this one having to do with home furnishings, and was soon working regularly four days a week on a free-lance basis at fifty dollars a day.

This meant that no taxes were withheld, so that even after paying the housekeeper, who came only during the afternoons, I was able to bank at least one hundred and twenty-five dollars a week.

My only extravagances were presents for the children. It made me so sad, especially on their birthdays, days that used to be such special occasions, to be off at work while Daddy was home drunk or God knows where, and to compensate, myself perhaps more than the boys, I bought whatever expensive toy or gadget they thought their hearts desired.

Working was good for me. It took my mind off my problems and gave me someplace to go and a sense of my own identity. The writing was challanging, so the days flew by, and even though the nights were still bad, they weren't as bad. I drank decidedly less so that I could be on the ball the following morning and was thus able to "maintain a more sympathetic and firm attitude," at least to the extent of not scrapping with Sean all evening. And he, in turn, when he was at all sober, tried to be helpful, telling the children that Mother had had a hard day and to do as they were told and pronto.

I especially liked the woman who had hired me. In addition to being bright and competent, Marjorie was a warm and sensitive person, and when we lunched as much time was spent discussing our children as office matters. I noticed that though she always encouraged me to have a drink or two, she never did. She said it made her sleepy. I never mentioned the fact that my husband was an alcoholic.

Nor did I ever mention this to my housekeeper. I didn't have to, because Alice and I understood each other. We were both trying to cope with problems we couldn't quite handle—in her case, an invalid husband; a daughter who had moved in with a Puerto Rican, an alliance of which she, as a black, disapproved; a continuing battle with her landlord; and an ongoing state of poverty caused primarily by her husband's ongoing need of expensive medications. Eschewing welfare, she instead held down as many jobs as she could manage. She came to our apartment in the afternoon, and as she left at six and I rarely was home before six-thirty, most of our communication was by phone. Sometimes she'd mention that my husband was home "resting," and we both knew what she meant. In fact, Alice not only knew; she knew the nuances.

One cold rainy night I came home, tired from a hard day, laden with groceries and very much in need of a restorative to get me launched into the evening shift. My AA literature to the contrary, I had taken to hiding a bottle, not Sean's bottle but my own bottle, so that I could be assured of having one drink at night. Sean, who was likely to drink up whatever was around, was on to what I was doing, so I kept shifting the hiding place, and the night before had carefully tucked my Scotch into one of the children's galoshes, not considering the possibility of rain.

When I came home I found all the galoshes drying on a newspaper on the kitchen floor, Alice having dutifully made the children wear them. A quick search through the closets and cabinets yielded no Scotch. I quietly called Alice's home, not quite knowing how to broach the subject without sounding considerably craven myself. However, as soon as I started to talk she interrupted to say that she had put my bottle on the top pantry shelf with the Christmas-tree lights, where she was sure I would find it untouched.

At the end of the year I had saved $4,000, and I began to think of making a break. This time I wanted to make sure there was no way, financially or psychologically, I could be coerced into returning.

However, at the end of the same year I had begun to experience times when my whole body shook uncontrollably, as if I had a violent case of the shivers. This happened once when I was lunching with my boss, my arm trembling so that I could hardly get my drink up to my mouth. I was afraid she might think I was an alcoholic and lamely said I had been drinking too much coffee, but she said she thought it was probably a case of nerves. I wondered if it was symptomatic of the change of life, as I was also having heavy night sweats, waking up wringing wet and in a turmoil.

I went to my gynecologist, the man who had delivered our four babies, a first-rate doctor, another of our Park Avenue practitioners, a brisk, dignified man, friendly but hardly a father-confessor type. I told him about the shakes and the sweats, but I couldn't get myself to mention Sean's drinking. It really didn't have anything to do with my uterus, which he said was splendid. I was, he added, a long way off from the change of life. As for the sweating, perhaps I was sleeping under too many covers, and unquestionably I should stop smoking and cut down on the coffee consumption.

So there was nothing wrong with me, physically, that couldn't be cured by peace and quiet, and yet, having become used to the way we lived, a now continually intoxicated husband (the friendly partnership had blown to pieces, and Bill was suing Sean for the costs of furnishing the splendid office), four increasingly nervous children, a demanding job, no social life or any other escape hatch, I couldn't figure out how to galvanize myself into action, to make the move that would rectify the situation.

Throughout Sean's illness I continually felt trapped between my love for him and my love and responsibility for our children. I knew I could manage them better if their alcoholic father were not around, and conversely I believed I could have been more understanding, sympathetic and firm—and thus possibly more helpful to his recovery—if I did not have to consider the boys. At least I could have just continued to love him were it not for the complications of trying to protect the children at the same time. Or, failing love, I could easily have left him and started a new life. I knew I could support myself. It was supporting and starting a new life for the children that was the hangup.

I had investigated renting another apartment, which I believed I could pay for if I continued to work, but I knew that the moment I left him Sean would march on my office and make my working too difficult for all concerned.

Just as the *Primer* had said, Sean's alcoholism was growing more "virulent . . . driving its victim[s] further and further from the normal world." He began to mumble about the "Krauts" and "Russkies" who were after him and increasingly accused me of ruining his career and plotting against him. Knowing the progression of his disease didn't make his talk any less frightening nor his disintegration any less painful to watch. He assured me that if I "tried anything" he would kill me on the spot, as he now personally had nothing to lose in so doing.

"You're all my life, all I've got left," he'd add softly. Sometimes this made the tears come to my eyes. He liked that and would reach out to hold my hand. Other times I'd say, "Please, darling, go see a doctor," but he didn't like that. It made him angry, as if I had insulted him.

Though I was convinced he would never harm the children, I knew he might well go to their schools and make a terrible scene or even spirit them away. (In a strange way, they, like me, were rather mesmerized by Sean, and he still had his kind of charismatic control over them.) I was dealing with a desperate man, and the strain and sadness of our life had made me paranoid, too. My fears were such that the only solution I could envisage was to run away and stay away until I could legally get Sean out of the apartment and out of our lives. Running away meant taking the children out of their schools and out of town, completely disrupting the continuity I wanted to maintain. But there were no alternatives, and knowing that with four children, or even with one, it's never the right time to do anything drastic, I decided the best time would be over the Christmas holidays. At least they would miss less school that way; and I couldn't face another drunken Christmas Day and dinner.

Early in November I went to see my divorce-mill lawyer.

Sitting in the reception room, I noticed that nothing had changed in the last year and a half—the same slick decor with the phony driftwood lamps, the same busty receptionist with her dyed black hair and rhinestone-trimmed harlequin glasses, busily directing office traffic with her nasal "honeys" and "dears" randomly disposed on clients and messenger boys alike. Everything was exactly the same except me. This time I didn't feel fragile. I felt firmly committed, intent on following through, and when we met, Bert immediately sensed the difference. He listened for ten minutes and then said, "This is going to cost you a minimum of fifteen hundred plus costs, with six hundred down before we serve the initial papers."

During my original series of visits he had never once mentioned fees.

In terms of the $25,000 Bill had spent to get rid of his alcoholic wife, $1,500 was a bargain, but it was still a big chunk out of my $4,000 dollars. Being hopeless as a haggler, and with no time to go ferreting out cheaper counsel, I wrote out a check for $600, postdated to my proposed day of departure. He agreed with my running-away plan and advised me against tying myself down to a lease on another apartment, saying he was sure he could get possession of ours in a matter of weeks, as, according to my description of Sean's condition, he wouldn't be so adroit this time in circumventing my rights.

"In fact," he added knowingly, "he'll probably be relieved when you make the move. He knows as well as you that this can't go on, and it's like waiting for the other shoe to drop. Perhaps when he gets off by himself he can work things out and pull himself together."

And then he asked the same question that was to be asked by future lawyers. I never knew whether it came up purely out of curiosity or a latent desire to play Masters and Johnson. It was such a simplistic question.

"It's a shame," he began. "Here's a guy with the best education, brains, top jobs, an attractive wife—and it's obvious you still love him or you wouldn't put up with this crap. Four kids, all the right credentials, and then suddenly he starts drinking himself out of business. Was there something wrong? I mean, well, what about your sex life? Problems?"

"Our sex life?" I asked, surprised. Why did he think I still loved my husband if on top of all the other problems we had been sexually incompatible? Sean was my first and only real lover and the best I could have asked for: passionate, sensitive, patient, solicitous, endearing, charming, amusing, natural, frank, and there had never been any shyness or pretense between us, nor, to my knowledge, any creeping monotony. If there was a problem in our sex life, I never knew about it, even now. I had read that alcoholics often became impotent, but that wasn't true in Sean's case.

As I well knew, the world's best cure for a hangover was the abandoned, lazy sensuality that—obliterating all pain—gradually gathers momentum for the delicious release of orgasm. After Sean became alcoholic, and by and large was continually hung over and was thus by and large continually seeking the cure, especially as he had little else to occupy his time and mind, sex turned into an issue, a rallying point for accusations rather than affection. I no longer wanted to kiss him, not because of the lips-that-touch-likker adage but because I couldn't stand the suffocating smell of gin. Sean would then accuse me of being cold and unresponsive and pronounce this the root cause of his drinking.

At one point I told him that if that were the problem, there was an easy solution, and that if he would stay sober, we'd make love twice a day. The program worked beautifully for four days, and then alcohol once again took precedence over my charms.

But being called frigid hurt, so I in turn would tell him that drink had made him a rotten lover. Yet at other times I would willingly copulate (it was rarely an act of love), because, drunk or sober, he could still satisfy me, and though the aesthetics were gone, the hunger remained. Sometimes I felt depraved. Other times, when our eyes would meet and I'd see a flicker of the former tenderness, I'd sink into the lowest depths of post-coital tristesse. I didn't know which of us was the most hurt and confused.

"No," I answered, looking at the framed picture of my lawyer's matronly wife and wondering if she loved him best because he was terrific in bed or because he had bought her a house in Scarsdale, "our sex life isn't the problem. The problem is that he's an alcoholic and there's no way to help him stop drinking. That's what's messed everything up."

Running Away

In the hopes of turning our fugitive flight into a holiday, I decided to run away to Florida, where the sun and the sea and the novelty of being in the tropics would lessen the strain of hiding out. I wanted the boys to have a good time, and I felt desperately in need of a vacation, some time off from trouble. This meant covering our traces completely so that Sean couldn't find us, even with the help of private detectives.

A woman traveling with four sons, all of whom were said to look alike, would be readily remembered by conductors, stewardesses or ticket takers on any public transportation. Going by car was out, as we had left ours in the country on blocks for the winter, and renting one meant giving my driver's license information and other easily traceable data. Renting was also the most expensive way to travel. I wasn't up to shipping the children off in different planes, trains or buses, and I felt it would be bad for them psychologically. The simplest solution was to fly together, and I made a reservation for Mr. and Mrs. Assumed Name and three children, but on a plane leaving from Philadelphia rather than New York.

I called a friend whose sister lived near Miami and asked if the latter would rent a house for me, but not in my name, for a month, thus avoiding registering at a hotel. She agreed with alacrity, saying that I was doing the right thing and that she and her husband would back me (he was an extremely wealthy man) and would arrange transportation to Philadelphia. I told one other close friend (so that I could stash clothes at her apartment) but no one else, neither my family nor the children.

Two weeks before we were to leave I had lunch with my boss to tell her not where I was going but why. I wanted to thank her for hiring me and and making the escape possible, and though I had never once mentioned Sean's drinking, I was sure she would understand and accept it as justification for my abrupt departure.

To my astonishment she said she had known all along and in the circumstances didn't know how I had managed to do so well by both the job and the children. "It's a tragic problem," she said quietly, "but you mustn't feel guilty about what you're doing." And then after saying that, when my marital problems were resolved, we'd talk about a full-time job with the firm, she insisted that I see a friend of hers at the national headquarters of AA. "She'll help you realize you're doing the right thing." Marjorie spoke with such restraint and conviction and without any of the party shibboleths that it was another year before I realized that she herself had been an alcoholic.

The AA executive was a very attractive, well-groomed woman who, in a brisk, no-nonsense manner, immediately told me she had joined AA twenty years ago after a long period of living and acting like a tramp. The words came out of her mouth like a tape recording, and in the same almost depersonalized way she went on: "It's an incurable disease, like diabetes. Help is available, but if your husband wants to go about his drinking, messing up the house, not taking care of himself, then you don't have to put up with it. You can't help him, so at least save the five of you. He's the only one who can save himself. You certainly cannot. And be sure to protect yourself with a good legal separation."

She further advised me not to tell his family, as it would take away the impact of my departure and, moreover, upset them. (Why, I wondered, shouldn't they be upset? He was their brother as well as my husband, although, by and large, they had turned their backs on the problem, as if I were his only keeper.)

Even though I questioned her doctrinaire do-it-yourself thinking, her forthright approval of my running-away plan—and she had obviously heard many other such plans—gave me courage. She was AA and she was saying, just as the psychiatrist had, "save yourself" and not the iffy "sometimes it may be necessary to take drastic action."

On the morning of departure I quietly told the two older boys that we were leaving Daddy for good and that the oldest, Sean, was to bring the two younger ones at noon from school to my friend's apartment and the thirteen-year-old, Curtis, was to come directly there from his school. Young Sean nodded solemnly, but Curtis said he felt he should stick around in case I had problems with Dad. I said absolutely not. If there were to be problems, I could handle them better alone. And, although I didn't say so, as I was leaving Sean for good, I wanted this to be a private, albeit secret and one-sided, farewell. By eight-fifteen the boys had gone, and Sean and I were alone in the apartment.

He was lying on his back in bed, the sheet pulled across his swollen stomach, one arm flung across his eyes, the other lying limply beside him. I tiptoed around, laying out clothes as if they were to go to the cleaners and putting shoes in a shopping bag as if they were to go to the shoemaker.

"What are you doing? he asked softly, sullenly.

"Just some errands, the cleaners—on the way to work." And

111

then once again, because he looked so pale and puffy and sick, I added, "Please, please go see a doctor. Promise me you'll go see a doctor. Go today."

"I don't need a doctor," he said. "I only need you."

"I think maybe what you need is a new woman," I answered, trying to make a little joke but wondering who it was that would take my place in our bed.

"Never," he said with a spark of his old decisiveness and a trace of his one-sided grin.

There was no substitute lover waiting for me in the wings, and I knew it would be a long time, maybe a lifetime, before I would ever be so close to anyone again. I took off my robe and lay down beside him. This was the goodbye I wanted, bloated belly, gin breath, and all.

Whether it was because the booze was finally bearing in on him or because he knew, the way he had always known, when there was something bothering or distracting me, my always passionate lover was impotent. We both became self-conscious, almost embarrassed by our futile fondling, and after a while I said I had to get dressed and go to work. (By work I meant the savings bank, to get my money and run.)

"Whore," he said sullenly, turning to pour himself a drink from the bottle beside the bed. Just as I was about to leave he charged out of the bedroom and, snatching the clothes out of my hands, jumped up and down in front of me, screaming over and over, "Get out of my life, you bitch, rotten wife, out, out, out!"

Curtis was waiting for me in the lobby. "I decided you might need me after all," he said quietly. "What about our clothes?"

"We'll just have to leave without them," I answered, still shaking from Sean's rage.

"I'll get them," he said confidently. "I'll tell Daddy I'm sick and got excused from school and then when he passes out again I'll bring them down. Don't worry, I can handle him." I nodded, sick and despairing of the damage already done. Our son was plotting and scheming against his father, just as I was, acting the little man but for all the wrong reasons.

When I returned from the bank he was standing in the doorway of the service entrance, saying he had everything downstairs in the basement but to hurry, as Daddy was getting dressed. As my lawyer had instructed, I gave the super a note to deliver to the apartment saying I was taking the children on a vacation and instituting separation proceedings so that Sean couldn't accuse me of kidnapping them. Then Curtis and I picked up the clothes and ran off down the street, a couple of criminals on the fly.

We met the other children at my friend's, and I told the boys we were going to take a trip, a holiday, and the prospect of coconuts, alligators and swimming in the middle of winter took some of the edge off their wide-eyed apprehension. The friend who had arranged the house in Florida came by and said that the car was downstairs and that we'd better get started. She handed me an envelope, saying it was a Christmas present from her husband. In it were five one-hundred-dollar bills. We collected our suitcases and shopping bags and piled into the elevator. We three adults tried to be very cheerful, but the boys were silent, worried and confused by the starkness and suddenness of leaving their accustomed world. And then they saw the car.

Throughout Sean's illness many friends did many warm and wonderful things for us, but this was one of the nicest. The car was a great, long, shiny black limousine, complete with liveried chauffeur and fur lap robe. We were on the lam, but we were going in style, and as we rolled down Fifth Avenue we all laughed at our amazing adventure.

"I feel like a movie star," Curtis said, his eyes shining, and Seamus said he hoped someone would see us. Then Nicholas, the quiet one, said pensively, "What will Daddy do about Christmas?"

"He'll be all right," I lied as carefully as I could, knowing

Sean was a desperately vulnerable and sick man and that something terrible and frightening was bound to happen to him.

Our hideaway house was perfect, an old rambling pine villa set back on an out-of-the-way street, obscured by dense tropical plants and trees and next door to my friend's sister's house. Jean had children of comparable ages, so the boys had instant pals and I had the comfort and support of their wonderful hospitality. They were determined that we would not feel marooned or lonely and had us over constantly. It had been so long since I had been in a normal home environment that I used to sit in their living room in a state of awe at the gentle, purposeful way they conducted their lives. Five days a week the husband went off to work in the morning and regularly returned at six in the evening, at which time he and his wife were genuinely glad to see each other again. Their evening ritual of cocktails always had the air of a little celebration, a homecoming, with the children sometimes joining in the conversation rather than inevitably seeking asylum in the television room as our boys had regularly done at home.

Jean and her husband took me to their holiday parties—they were very attractive and popular—and sometimes they got a bit high, but they never became drunk, and it was almost disorienting to be out socializing again, especially so because I didn't have a drunken husband to worry about. I wanted to relax and have fun, but it was difficult. I didn't want to explain who I was or why I was there or what I had left behind, and pretending that Sean had never existed made me feel too anonymous, even deceitful. I couldn't stop worrying about him, and between that and the accumulated exhaustion of the past two years I often awoke in the middle of the night in tears.

Overall, however, our escape was a total success in every way but one: Nothing was happening legally. We had left early in December, and just before Christmas I received a letter from Bert saying that, according to the superintendent, my husband had left town so that the process server had been unable to do his thing.

The letter also noted that my six-hundred-dollar check (which I had postdated to the date of my departure) had bounced and would have to be covered before his office could proceed. In plotting my escape I had carefully left the exact amount in my checking account, never dreaming that Sean would wipe it out by forging my signature on one of the checks I had left behind.

Money was disappearing much faster than I had dreamed possible. Plane fares, Christmas presents, car rental, food, trips to the Sequarium, Serpentarium, Everglades, and now another six hundred to the lawyer, and somehow twenty-two hundred was gone. I called Bert to find he was taking the holiday week off, and another ten days went by before I could reach him.

"Look, dear," his disembodied voice said over the phone, "this is going to go on and on, I'm afraid. We just can't find him, and the only alternative is to publish a notice in the papers, but that will cost a helluva lot of dough and won't get you the apartment in time for school—he's had the locks changed again—and that means hotels and more money and I think you'd be much better off if you stay down there, put the kids in school and get a job until we get this mess straightened out. It's going to be rough if you come back—and besides," he finished with irritating good humor, "six months in Florida sounds great to me!"

I asked the boys how they felt about staying, and they were adamantly against it. The novelty had worn off and they were itchy to return home. My night sweats and the shaking, which I now realized had been the result of tension, had virtually stopped, and I felt rested and up to fighting it out; so I packed up and made plane reservations to leave in two days when the rental on our house would be up. But just to be on the safe side, I spent the first of those two days looking at available houses, only to find they were few and far between and, it being the height of the season, very expensive.

As we had no telephone in our house, I went to Jean's to call Bert and tell him I was returning. As I was dialing she mentioned that I had received a call earlier from someone who said she was a friend of my father's and anxious to get in touch with me. I hung up the phone, and my paranoia was instantly back. I knew that the call was from a private detective and that Sean had tracked us down.

If there was any positive aspect to living with an alcoholic, it was learning to accommodate feelings of panic: take a deep breath, separate the essential problem from the ones that were peripheral to it, evaluate the options, make a decision, and act quickly. The super of our apartment was an honest man, and he'd said Sean was out of town, which meant he could be in Miami. To make sure I wasn't fantasizing, I called my father, who confirmed my fears, saying that of course he hadn't asked anyone to call me. "Be careful, darling," he said. "He's called here looking for you, and he sounds like he is out of his head."

It was one thing to be in Florida and think I was rested and ready to do battle with my alcoholic, and it was another to feel his presence close by. The essential thing was to stay away from him, and this wouldn't be possible in New York, as Sean would make it his business to find us as soon as the children were back in school. I called the real-estate agent and told him I would take one of the houses, provided I could move in that very afternoon. He agreed. I went back to our discovered hideaway, told the boys to pack the car and that we were moving into another house and staying on.

"What!" they protested as one. "You said we could go home. We hate it here." I quietly told them that Daddy knew where we were but wouldn't find us if we moved to another house, and if we returned to New York we'd be right back where we started. That prospect was too much for them, too, and they immediately started loading up the car.

"We're getting good at this," young Sean said, smiling.

"At what?" I asked.

"At running away and hiding," he answered.

We moved in that night, and I returned the rented car, telling the clerk several times that I was leaving that night for New York. After we were settled in our new house I learned that my paranoia was substantiated. Jean said a man had come to her door asking for us; she had said we had returned to New York, and he hadn't been heard from since. I had gambled on the assumption that private eyes do sloppy work and that Sean was too drunk to press the search. But the fear lingered on, and for the next several weeks, though I knew I should be out looking for a job, I stayed inside, the door bolted, and whenever a car or a pedestrian slowed down in front of the house I was sure it was another detective, and the shaking and sweating returned.

We stayed in Florida five months, and during that time I learned several valuable lessons, the main one being that trying to resolve the major problem of my life by running away from it was an exercise in futility. I never received a single scrap of paper that made me legally separated from my husband, and I never spent a single day without the anguish of still loving him—a longing for the relationship that once was and constant, gnawing, gut feeling that he needed me and I had let him down.

My head—and my family and friends—told me that it was time to shuck off the morbidity of the past several years and start a new life—forget the past, enjoy the present, program a better future. It was the right idea but easier said than done.

The future got off to a good start. The second house was pleasant, the weather was gorgeous, a social life evolved through my friends, Jean and her husband, and soon I even had the most necessary accessory for a new life, an escort, a boyfriend. He was a pro at courting women, a thrice-divorced swinger, an excellent dancer, the best restaurants, a snappy foreign car, not a dynamic conversationalist but amusing and sweet. At first I relished my new-found image, riding around in an open car, hair blowing in the breeze, cha-cha-chaing and drinking champagne, a rejuvenated middle-aged playgirl. But it was my image, not his, that interested me, and as the practical exigencies of my new life combined with the stark and painful truths of the old continued to loom intractably, my interest in trying to play the playgirl paled. There were more pressing concerns, both financial and psychological.

I felt uncomfortable going out with another man, in part because of the children. Their father had meant too much to them and they were too young, too bewildered, to accept my need or right to a physical relationship with a stranger. And I, too, was still committed to my married state. My lawyer had warned me to stay as pure as Caesar's wife until I was legally separated, but even if he hadn't, a surreptitious sex life would have made me feel like a cheat. I really didn't want a boyfriend, a mere playmate and lover. I needed a surrogate husband with whom I could share my problems.

Having never had the responsibility of supporting four children, I had forged ahead on the assumption that I could (and also on the assumption that I would in due course receive child support) without changing the economic format of their lives. In addition to signing a five-month lease for a monthly rental of three hundred and fifty dollars, I had enrolled the children in private schools, convinced they would do better academically there than in the unfamiliar ambiance of a large public school then in the throes of integration. (It was the throes, not the integration, that bothered me, as their New York school had always had black students.)

I had also assumed that because I had been able to earn fifty dollars a day in highly competitive New York, finding a job in Miami would be duck soup. I didn't realize that the town was full of people like myself, refugees from the North, many with far better résumés than I could produce. I made the rounds of agencies, newspapers, department stores, radio stations, hotels, any and everything remotely connected with public relations, inevitably to hear that there were no openings at this time. Gradually it dawned on me that whatever my skills, my situation was patently clear and familiar: a woman on the fly, unrooted, here today and gone tomorrow, a poor job risk.

The search was further complicated by not having a car. After I turned in the rented one, I decided that we could make do on bikes and used one of the four secondhand ones I had bought the boys to market and go to the laundromat. I learned to balance the heavy loads on the side baskets and told myself it was good exercise, rain or shine, and that people didn't need cars; but when I started to look for a job, I discovered that in Miami people did. Everyone, from fourteen-year-olds to the lame and the halt, drove. Public transportation was, for all practical purposes, nonexistent. The buses were few and far between and the routes serpentined endlessly, so that a twenty-minute car ride turned into a two-hour bus expedition. I finally gave up and bought a four-hundred-dollar station wagon; but even that didn't help me get a job.

When the day came that I had thirty-eight dollars in my checking account I got in the car and drove to downtown Miami and the U.S. Employment Bureau, prepared to take any job short of a topless dancer. I was the only white person present among the ranks of the unemployed, and that was a bad sign. If the blacks couldn't get jobs as underpaid housemaids or other menial work, there was little hope for a white applicant at whatever nominal salary. I saw a sign that said, incongruously, "Executive Placement," and went over to the desk where a man sat reading a newspaper.

He gave me a quizzical look and then invited me to sit down and began shuffling through the few cards in his file box, shaking his head, saying that two months ago there was a listing that would have suited me to a "T." "Bad time of the year, I'm afraid. Weather's good. I don't understand it," he empathized. "It's a shame, you and four kids. I'll make sure and call you first thing that comes up." I thanked him and left, at a loss as to what to do next. Just as I reached the door he ran after me. "Try the university," he said. "Sometimes they're looking for people. It's worth a try anyway."

Keep digging, don't quit, be a good Bennington girl, and sure enough, after three interviews in which I said I was divorced and hoped to remain in Florida for the rest of my life, the sun broke through at Sunshine U, and I was hired as the development writer for one hundred and sixty-five dollars a week. We celebrated by going to dinner and splurging on Jumbo Super Burgers and Giant Slurpies.

My salary barely covered rent and food, with nothing left for doctors, dentists, clothes, the usual expenses of four children, let alone any extra money for recreation. (With no television and no money for movies, we all settled for riding bikes and visiting the local library.) I didn't know how I was going to make ends meet, and so, swallowing my pride, I wrote my father, my sister's husband and Sean's brothers, asking for financial help. I tried to present my predicament in the most practical, objective terms— the unfortunate fact of their father's illness didn't mitigate his children's needs—but nonetheless they were begging letters. My father and sister's husband immediately called to say they'd send a monthly check, and Sean's brother Dan sent six hundred dollars and a heart-warming note saying he should have realized my dilemma and would henceforth mail a check each month. (Dan was the boys' favorite uncle, a winning, bright, reassuring man, and they felt immensely bolstered to learn their father's brother cared so much for their well-being.) But Sean's other brother never answered my letter. This hurt, not because of the money but because his silence made me think he blamed me for Sean's illness and, blaming me, didn't give a damn about "my" children. Alcoholism is fraught with misunderstanding, and this leads to estrangment.

In the middle of February I received a call from Dan telling me that Sean was in Bellevue, out of his mind and critically ill with a liver failure. Alone and drunk in our apartment, he saw men coming through the ninth-floor windows, armed and wearing gas masks. He called a former associate in the U. S. Attorney's office, an old friend who was now a city commissioner, to report the invasion, and the friend sent two policemen to the apartment. Off my alcoholic went to the wards. It was just like *The Lost Weekend*, just as unbelievable but far worse because it was my husband for real and not Ray Milland in the movies; and yet there was a ghastly logic in the horror of what was happening to Sean, an inevitable progression. I was preconditioned to accept the fact that Bellevue was what happened to alcoholics.

My first reaction was to return to him immediately. This had to be "the bottom," and he would need all the love and help I could give him to start the climb back up. But there were practical problems. It meant snatching the children out of school again and plunking them back down in emotional chaos, of forfeiting the thousand I had paid in tuition (and the remainder due in the contract), the seven hundred I had paid on my rented house (and the thousand dollars due for the next three months). Perhaps it would be better to let Sean work his way back up alone, without adding to his confused state the conflicts of our own complicated relationship. He was bound to feel bitterness toward me, and if he were out of his mind, my presence could understandably jar rather than soothe him.

I called one of our doctor friends and he concurred, saying he believed my husband would live and was making arrangements to transfer him to a private hospital, where he would receive the best medical care, the key to his recuperation. And I spoke to my lawyer, who said I definitely should not return until I had a clearer picture of the future. He also told me that he had sent the process server to Bellevue and that my husband, theoretically at death's door, had beaten him up and would I send another fifty dollars to cover the process server's doctor's bill. (Sean hadn't lost the bravura I liked, and I admired him for fighting back at the countdown.) I asked Bert how the service could possibly stand up in court. He said he thought it would, but of course it didn't, and ultimately that caused further delays.

During his subsequent hospitalization after Bellevue, Sean had several sessions with a young psychiatrist, and the psychiatrist reported to Dan, who reported it to me, that his patient had, "for want of a better word, grandiosity," and it was "doubtful" that he would ever get over it or his concomitant compulsion to drink. Thus, even Bellevue wasn't the bottom; in fact, for Sean there was to be no bottom. After only a few sessions the young psychiatrist was able to determine that my husband was a hopeless case, psychiatrically, alcoholically, and, therefore, physically.

I went to the library and looked for "grandiosity" in the medical dictionaries. I found "grandiose"—characterized by showing feelings of great importance—and, in another, characterized by a feeling of being important, wealthy or influential, where there is no basis for such feeling.

So now I knew what had made my husband an alcoholic. Or did I? Why did Sean's feeling of self-importance manifest itself as a compulsion to drink rather than run for political office or star in the movies? There had to be a touch of grandiosity in anyone who had the guts to impose himself on the public, to make the basically arbitrary decision that one personally was better equipped and better suited to leadership than another. What about Lyndon Johnson? Or Shirley Temple? Or Ronald Reagan? My husband had been a leader from his childhood onward, and as he had said in a letter written to his brother from Camp Claiborne, before he went overseas:

> I have confidence in myself, and "in the stars" and I know that whatever happens to me from here on in will only be to my advantage.

Why did this grandiose confidence, which in the context of the time and situation could well be interpreted as bravery, take such a negative turn?

I recalled that when we were in Europe on the second trip and were gluing ourselves back together with a pre-luncheon Fernet Branca after a long night of bubbles and eggs, Sean had said philosophically—and again with a touch of bravura—"I've decided I'm lucky. I've outlived my father, which I never expected to do, and everything is working the way I wanted it to." Deciding he was lucky, not being humble, must have been another warning of his grandiosity. But maybe, deep down, he only meant that he was lucky to have outlived his father, not to die at thirty-three; perhaps he never adjusted to the shock and was still scared and trying to bluff through his fear. When he was drunk he dramatized, fantasized his role of marked man, convinced that the "Russkies" and "Krauts" were after him and that armed men in gas masks were outside the window when he went off to Bellevue. Though I hadn't been able to understand the depth of Sean's bitterness, his sense of feeling gypped, when we were courting, I could far better understand it now as I saw the effect his alcoholism was having on our children. It was bound to leave an indelible, lifelong wound.

Conceivably the young psychiatrist meant to probe a little deeper but couldn't, because at the end of a month Sean left the hospital. He was told that he had cirrhosis and must not drink again, and that was the end of his treatment. And, according to a few friends who had seen him, the treatment wasn't really effective. Sean spoke of his hospitalization in terms of a physical illness that had nothing to do with alcoholism other than that from now on he could drink only moderately.

The prognosis, then, was bad. I remained firm in my quest for a separation, assuming that for the time being, at least, he would be sufficiently scared into sobriety to give proper recognition to my suit. I continued to wait for something to happen, and in the middle of April, five months after I had left New York, my lawyer finally met Sean in court.

Bert had said he'd call immediately to give me a progress report. When he did, I was shattered. He told me that nothing

123

happened because my husband, who appeared as his own counsel, was tight and too disoriented to answer the simplest, most routine questions, and the judge had put the hearing off until my husband could be properly represented.

"It was tragic," Bert said, with genuine sadness in his voice. "He was totally confused, not angry, not even really drunk, more like he was out of his mind, just kept saying, as if he didn't understand why we were in court, 'She's my wife.' " He added that he was trying to contact a lawyer friend of Sean's who could act on his behalf so that we could proceed. I hung up and burst into tears. Was there no end to the sadness, no resolution for his problems or mine?

Substantively, my new life was a flop. We had all come to loathe living in Florida and, despite new friends, still felt like strangers hiding out in a strange land, one that was becoming suffocatingly hot and humid. We had only enough money to get by and not enough for diversion. We were being sustained by monthly handouts, which I knew couldn't continue indefinitely, just as I knew that Sean must be making deep inroads into his own assets. The longer it took to reach a separation agreement, the less there would be for a settlement. I learned that he had given up our three-bedroom rent-controlled apartment and taken a small one off Fifth Avenue, so that meant home base was now wiped out. With the prospect of child support growing more dim daily, the only realistic change I could envision in our life style was to keep lowering it, stick it out in Florida, move to a cheaper neighborhood, send the children to public schools.

They had been wonderfully good sports and tried very hard to like their new life, but they couldn't help persisting in asking when we could go home. I knew they were not happy. After a long day's work at a job that bored me, I'd sit on our patio, no less hot and humid than our nonair-conditioned house, watching those obscene little lizards darting across the white stucco walls, sipping a drink in which the ice melted instantly and the glass sweated in rivulets, wondering what I had accomplished in running away.

During our five months in Florida I made a point of going to Mass every Sunday and of making the children go too. I felt we all needed the reassurance that God was love and this was the essence that gave order to life, the pattern and force that held the pieces together. We went to church the Sunday after I had talked to Bert, and while I was praying to God to help Sean it came to me that I must write and beg him to hospitalize himself again. The minute we returned home I wrote, saying we could discuss alternative plans after he was better and that the only thing that mattered was his recovery.

To avoid the Florida postmark, so that Sean wouldn't descend on us, I sent the letter to my lawyer to mail. He promptly returned it with a note to the effect that such a letter would jeopardize my case. I sent the letter off again. My so-called case (still nonexistent for all practical purposes) was meaningless in terms of my husband's life. I wrote Bert that it had to be mailed.

Thus I couldn't blame my lawyer when my secretary came in one morning late in May and said, "That's funny. Some man just called and asked if you were here, and when I said yes he hung up."

I was stunned but not surprised. That afternoon I looked out of my window and saw Sean. He had found me and, even if I ducked out, would inevitably find our house. As he was still my legal husband it would be pointless to try to rout him by calling the police. There was no place left to hide, and to avoid a scene in my office I went out to meet him.

He was thin and pale, and in his dark business suit and dark glasses he stood out, a furtive, ominous figure, amidst the casually dressed, suntanned students. Walking toward him, I realized that he was tight.

"Where are my children?" he asked menacingly. "You've kidnapped my children."

"The children are fine. How are you?" I answered as casually

125

as possible. He didn't answer, and I waited, not knowing what he would do or what I should do next. Then he took off his dark glasses and tears streamed from his eyes. "Please come back. If you don't come back to me I'll die."

I wasn't sure he could ever stop drinking, but I was sure I loved him too much not to give it a try; and, if he were going to die, I belonged by his side.

We left three days later, and it was glorious to be back in our own East Hampton home. Even had I had a legal separation, I think I would have done the same.

~10~

Playing God
Summer 1967

If I had been a psychiatrist or a member of AA or if we had gone off to live alone together on a desert island, our program might have worked. We agreed there would be no booze in the house, but instead lots of good food, love and quiet times so that he could build himself back up to return to work in the fall. In the beginning, coming together glossed over the six months' separation, as if it and the previous bad years had never happened; but as the days went by the emotional strains we had both endured began to surface. He couldn't help but ask me why I had deserted him, especially when he had been "thrown into Bellevue, with niggers kneeling on my chest, beating me," and there was no way I could explain my fears and tears and what had gone on in my heart and head. We couldn't talk without talking about the past, but he refused to talk about his drinking, so there was no way we could communicate. He mentioned being in Miami during the past winter, saying he had fallen in with bad companions, as if his presence there was a mere Pinocchio escapade, with no relevance to me, and I was afraid to rile the waters by asking how he found out where we were.

He looked better than he had in years, trim and tall, but he tired very easily, and this made him nervous and depressed and I, in turn, became very edgy. Gradually, the tension we were both trying to avoid began to build. I desperately longed to have one of my soothing nightly drinks and began to resent my enforced abstinence, and at the end of a month I made an egregious error: I asked Sean if it would bother him if I had a glass of wine with dinner. He said no, and two weeks later the round-the-clock drinking was back in full swing. I tried to tell myself that it might have happened anyway, but there was no way to rectify my mistake and no way to assuage my guilt. How, I asked myself over and over, could I have been so selfish and so stupid? After all we had both been through, I still couldn't understand what it meant to be an alcoholic. No one who hasn't been there can.

Almost overnight his skin turned a waxy yellow and the whites of his eyes a muddy saffron. There were little red pustules, the kind called angry, covering his back and chest—and he had an almost constant nosebleed, sometimes just a trickle, other times in a fairly heavy stream. His arms and legs got thinner and thinner and his stomach bigger and bigger until it became a tight round ball, as if he were eight months pregnant, with his navel distended like a baby bottle's rubber nipple.

He rarely bathed or shaved, spent most of the day sleeping, usually in bed but sometimes on the living-room couch or floor and sometimes on the lawn. When the children brought friends home and found their father stretched out across the living-room rug, they tried to ignore his presence, speaking in normal voices and stepping around him as their pals looked on, goggle-eyed. Only once did I hear a comment. Phil, a hulking six-foot-four fifteen-year-old who always filled up the room when he came in, stumbled across the prostrate figure and said, "Oh, sorry, sir."

Getting no response, he turned to young Sean and said with amazing tact, "Gosh, your father sure is tired."

In addition to being a very depressing sight, he was, as sick people often are, difficult and demanding, raging if the children played records loudly, yelling my name over and over when he wanted something, hiding the car keys so I couldn't leave the house unless he came along, no matter how drunk and disreputable, and insisting that I sleep in the same bed, where sleep was nearly impossible. (If I sought sanctuary in another room, he'd follow.) Sometimes I became angry, but most of the time I was in a tearful stupor. The psychiatrist had said he was a hopeless alcoholic and the doctors had said that if he continued to drink he would die, and as both prognostications were assumed irrefutable, he was, perforce, in the process of dying; and though his death would solve many problems, it was agonizing to watch the man I loved destroying himself. I felt overwhelmed, helpless, and my only comfort came from my belief that I had done the right thing in returning; at least he had the consolation of dying in his own home, with his family beside him.

On two occasions I called the doctor. One Sunday evening Sean was lying in bed, his face wincing in pain, a thin trickle of blood coming from his nose, and as I tiptoed about straightening the sheets it seemed to me that he was having difficulty breathing. I called the village medical center and asked for a doctor. A man I didn't know arrived, and as I met him at the door I quickly explained the previous liver failure. The weary doctor went upstairs with me and, penetrating the alcoholic gloom, asked my husband in a hearty, jovial voice how he was feeling. My husband answered, sadly and weakly, that he was feeling pretty bad.

"Well, we'll fix you up," the doctor said comfortingly. After examining Sean, the doctor prescribed vitamins and tranquilizers. "This will make you sleep," he said, giving him a shot. "And tomorrow you start the vitamins and tranquilizers. And try to lay off the brown stuff," he finished in a kind, fatherly voice.

I followed him downstairs, very grateful to him for coming late on Sunday night, so much more responsible than Dr. Pierce, who had refused to make a house call in New York. "How is he, really?" I asked, dreading the answer.

"His pulse and heart are strong, but his liver's very enlarged. It's an awful problem," he said, "and I know it's difficult on the family. Try to keep him off the brown stuff," he advised again, and then he smiled sympathetically and walked away through the dark to his car. I later learned that he was affiliated with the alcoholism department of the county mental health board.

We had a four-day recovery period. The shot kept him out for almost twenty-four hours, after which he told me he had had the worst nightmares of his life. He took the prescribed tranquilizers for three days, only to announce that they made him feel worse than his worst hangover, 100 percent crazy, dizzy, and somewhere other than in this world. So back came the bottle.

Two weeks later I called the clinic again and for the same reason: Sean's nose was bleeding; he moaned in pain and breathed in deep, intermittent sighs. I was convinced that he was dying and, except to go downstairs to cry, stayed by his side. I decided that the first doctor didn't know anything and asked for the doctor who, over the summers, had treated the children for cuts, sprains, poison ivy, and other seasonal maladies. He had trained at New York Hospital and I liked and respected him. As soon as he arrived I anxiously reeled off Sean's drinking history, and he gave me an understanding nod and then went upstairs to see the patient. He examined Sean briefly, gave him a shot, and told him to continue the vitamins and tranquilizers. I told him that the tranquilizers upset my husband; the doctor nodded and jotted off a prescription for a different kind.

Downstairs I asked how Sean really was. "His heart and pulse are fine, but the liver's very distended. Can't you get him to go away, to hospitalize himself for a while?" And he mentioned a drying-out clinic that was not too distant and not too expensive.

"I'll try," I said wearily, emotionally drained by my apparently absurd death watch. Obviously neither doctor considered my husband to be as sick as I believed. Or perhaps it was exactly as Dr. Pierce had said in New York, and there was nothing a doctor could do for my husband and the house calls were a waste of their time and our money.

For the next ten days I tried every approach I could think of to get Sean to hospitalize himself. I pleaded with him, for my sake, because I loved him and wanted him to get well, to go for a few days. I called the drying-out clinic and reported to him that it would cost only seventy-five dollars for four days or one hundred and twenty-five for a week. "You'll be more comfortable there," I begged. "They'll know what to give you, and then you won't need a drink."

At other times I would march into our bedroom, playing the brisk head nurse, and announce that he *had* to go to a hospital, that I could *not* take care of him, that his lying in bed and dying was very *bad* for the children and that he owed it to himself, to his four sons and to me to go forthwith. But whatever my approach, his answer was always the same.

"I hate hospitals. I will never go to a hospital—and you cannot get me to go to a hospital."

By the middle of August it seemed to me that, despite what the doctors said, the end was very near. He rarely left bed, refused to eat anything but a little potato salad and was too weak to get up. I fetched bedpans, kept changing the bloodstained sheets, and kept a bowl of ice on the bedside table to bathe his forehead.

Since he had started drinking six weeks earlier I had tried every wile to keep him away from the bottle. I hid his checkbook so he couldn't pay for deliveries, but the friendly liquor-store man willingly put the bottle on the bill. I intercepted deliveries only to have my husband make another call or go on a rampage until I forked it over. My alcoholism literature had warned me that such wiles wouldn't work, so finally I gave up. When I reminded him that the doctors had said he must not drink because of his cirrhosis, he'd turn away or sometimes smile his gentle one-sided grin. It was as if he wanted to die, to put an end to our unhappiness, to commit the final and only act left for a man of his integrity.

As he became weaker he began to ask me to make the calls for fresh supplies. Usually I'd say no, even though this made him very angry and upset, and eventually he'd gather the strength to make the call himself. Then I began to relent. If it was impossible to keep him from drinking himself to death, then the kindest role I could play was that of angel of mercy, even if it meant helping him to die.

At cocktail time I brought my own clean martini to his bedside (his bottle of gin had small clots of blood and phlegm floating in it) and listened to stories of his boyhood in New England or to tales of his missions as a secret agent in Berlin and Moscow. It didn't matter which of the stories were fact and which fantasy; they were all absolutely true to him, the agent stories being even more real because they were more recent than the childhood memories. Sometimes he'd suddenly turn off the light and put out his hand for silence, alerting me that the enemy was out in the adjacent potato field, laying for him. To protect himself, Sean kept a rifle with a telescopic sight under our bed. He had bought it when I was in Florida.

The gun worried me. Though I never thought he'd use it against me, I was afraid that the children would play around with it, even though he assured me that it was not loaded and that the bullets were hidden and that he would never let it out of his immediate control. At least the last point was true. I made several attempts to sneak it away and hide it, but he always found out immediately and made a room-to-room search until he got it back. It occurred to me to throw it in the bottom of the nearby lily pond, but this would be destroying another's property and, thus, wrong. In playing Cordelia to my husband's Lear, two birds locked into the certain knowledge of his absurdly inevitable death, I had become as confused and irrational as my alcoholic. The only difference was that I was sober and physically sound and he was neither.

One afternoon late in August I was sitting on the side stoop beneath our bedroom window, half listening for the imminent death rattle upstairs, watching an occasional sparrow or red-winged blackbird, tranquilized by the beautiful sweep of trees, the potato field and the dunes beyond—my kind of peace. Suddenly, from around the corner of our house, appeared one of my husband's oldest and best friends, a classmate at Williams, graduating *summa* to Sean's *cum laude,* and later a fellow student at Harvard, taking his degree in medicine. He was now a psychiatrist, and as he didn't practice in New York, we hadn't seen him for several years. I was surprised and delighted that he had come to visit, and while expressing my pleasure I heard the upstairs window shade snap up and Sean called out that he'd be down as soon as dressed.

I barely had time to explain to Dick, who knew about Sean's drinking, that my husband was now dying when the latter appeared, shaven, hair combed, clean tennis shorts and jacket and with his yellowed eyes hidden behind the ever-present dark glasses. Miraculously, he looked almost normal, even sound, and Dick gave me a puzzled look as Sean announced that the reunion called for a celebration. We walked to the trestle table in the back yard while the host went for gin and ice and vermouth.

For a brief while it was just like old times. We three had traveled together in Europe when Sean and Dick were at Harvard, and then and thereafter some of my favorite times had been spent in listening to the two of them talk. The Rose Window led to Henry James, which led to William James, which led to Spengler or Sartre and on to France and politics, *ad infinitum* and inexhaustibly, and all I had to do to be entertained was to sit and listen, with an occasional interjection to remind them that I was still present and conscious. So began our reunion, but in a short while my husband began to leave his thoughts in transit, and his body, back still straight, began to pitch and roll, side to side and front to back, and his glasses slid down his nose. Dick stopped short in the middle of a sentence.

"Good God, man," he said quietly and earnestly, "put yourself in a hospital for two years, otherwise you'll be dead in six months." My alcoholic hooted with laughter and, putting his head on the table, passed out.

That evening Dick said that my husband absolutely had to be hospitalized, even if it meant that I had to commit him. This was the first time anyone—doctors, lawyers, the AA men, family or friends—had indicated that there was a way to force Sean into hospitalization. Commitment was for the poor, the insane. The word had an ominous sound.

"Commit him where?" I asked suspiciously.

He mentioned private psychiatric hospitals but said the cost, around three thousand a month, was probably prohibitive, as Sean would need at least six months, or fifteen thousand worth, of treatment if it were to have any long-term effect.

"So," he said matter-of-factly, "if you can't afford that, you commit him to a state hospital. I don't know what the laws are in New York, but in my state we can put alcoholics away for two years. He won't get the best of care, but it's better to institutionalize him than to let him stay home and drink himself to death."

I had never been to a state mental hospital, and to me it was a remote place with barred windows where society's rejects, primarily poor people, were sent and forgotten. I suddenly recalled case histories in my alcoholic literature. "I was in and out of jails, institutions, Skid Row," as if they were all one and the same experience. And my mother-in-law's doctor's admonition: "We'll put you in the state institution, cockroaches and all."

"That sounds like a horrible idea," I said.

"Well, unless you think you're God, you can't just sit by and let him die—which he will do and very shortly," he answered, zeroing in on my fantasies.

The next day I called my doctor friends who lived in New York City but also summered in East Hampton. He was an internist and she a psychiatrist, and both had tried to help Sean. He had arranged his transfer out of Bellevue into a private hospital, and she had arranged his appointment with the drink-shrink the first time I left Sean. When the problems of his alcoholism got me down, I could always call on them for friendship and understanding, more than any other people. We arranged to meet, with Dick, for a secret conference at the beach as soon as Sean passed out. It was a gray, foggy day, and no one else was there. We could be out of earshot of either the patient or any of our respective children at home.

Both of my doctor friends concurred with Dick, saying my alcoholic was in desperate need of hospitalization, and they would help make the arrangements. The procedure involved getting two doctors to sign a paper attesting to the patient's need for commitment and then taking the paper to a judge to sign, after which my husband would be admitted to the state hospital for the prescribed period. In the case of alcoholics, it was possible to get a sixty-day commitment. As an out-of-state psychiatrist, Dick couldn't sign, and my New York friends said that as close friends they would prefer not to but would if I had difficulty finding local doctors to sign. I assured them this would not be necessary, as two local doctors were very much aware of Sean's condition, having recently examined him.

Before he left Dick said to me, "You know, it's not going to make that much difference if you do it tomorrow or within the next ten days. It's going to be difficult, so wait until you feel up to it. And don't commit him on a weekend when the hospital is on half staff. It might be twenty-four hours before a doctor gets around to him."

The next day I took my papers to the medical center and

asked the doctors who had seen Sean to sign them. To my astonishment, they both refused, adamantly and concisely. One said, "You know these are hopeless cases, don't you?" and the other, the one who was on the county board for alcoholism, said, "It won't do any good unless he wants to go."

Having seen the condition my alcoholic was in, I don't to this day know why they refused. Whatever the cause, he was a very sick human being, mentally and physically, suffering from malnutrition, a distended liver, and if they knew anything whatsoever about alcoholism, they must have known his mind was not in good working order. At this point any kind of hospitalization would have helped him—the one doctor had in fact suggested it —as well as giving a reprieve to me and the children.

Perhaps they had no faith in the healing powers of the state hospital, or perhaps they felt the hospital should minister only to less ignoble diseases; or perhaps, knowing that my husband was a lawyer, they didn't want to get in the position of being sued for malpractice. Whereas Dr. Pierce had made me feel I was telling him a family secret, these two had made me feel I was trying to do an evil deed.

I reported this to Jim and his wife, my medical friends from New York. They were not at all surprised and said they'd sign the papers but would wait until the very day Sean went to the hospital so he couldn't later claim that he'd been a little drunk during the week but completely sober the day he was kidnapped off to the mental institution.

"You know," I told them morosely, "he's never going to agree to go, and he'll fight off anyone who tries to take him." Jim, who is one of the most responsible and kind men I have ever known, nodded and said there were always people available to take him, forcibly if necessary, and that he had already looked into the situation for me. He gave me the number of a local policeman who did this kind of "work" when off duty, and I called from their house to learn that he was free the very next day or four days later and that his fee for driving my husband to the state hospital, some sixty miles away, was fifty dollars. I had recently received a check for three hundred from the sale of the station wagon I had bought in Florida and, anxious to get the whole humiliating process over as quickly as possible, agreed on the fee and set the date for the following day.

"How will you get him to come with you?" I asked. He said he would bring an assistant and that both of them had done a lot of this kind of work and would be very gentle.

"Yes, but how will you get him to come with you?" I repeated.

"Well, if necessary, we'll use a camisole," he said blandly.

"You mean a strait jacket, don't you?" I demanded.

"Yes, but this is the newest kind of camisole. It's much softer and more comfortable than the old ones."

I was horrified and sickened. My handsome, my bright, tender husband, trussed up like a pig. I told him not to come.

Neither Jim nor his wife made any comment when I told them I had chickened out. I went to the beach for the afternoon, relieved that I had made the decision. Maybe, somehow, the problem would go away before I had to do anything so degrading, either to Sean or to myself.

But of course it didn't go away. It only got worse. In addition to the rifle he now kept his hatchet beside him and wouldn't allow the light to be turned on because "they" were out in the potato field. At times his hands shook uncontrollably, and occasionally one arm flapped like the wing of a dying chicken. He constantly had the dry heaves and said he was going crazy from being so constipated; and because he had neither bathed nor shaved in days, the whole room smelled, a sweet, sickly odor of decay. I kept thinking about the strait jacket.

Worried that I really would be doing an inhuman and evil act, I called one of Sean's friends, now vacationing in East Hampton. He was a partner in the law firm Sean had worked for when we returned from Washington, and I asked him if he would read the commitment papers, saying I wasn't clear as to what they really meant. If I were doing wrong, he'd be in the position of telling me so and also of protecting my husband.

"I'm afraid it's all too clear," he said, reading them, "but there's nothing else you can do. It's really terrible. He's such a fine guy and a good lawyer, but he's made a godawful mess of his life and yours and your kids." And then, with the practical insight of the true trouble-shooter, he added, "Actually, it's a shame he doesn't get hit by a truck."

He meant it sympathetically, to avoid all the rottenness of what was to come, but it reflected the negative view toward alcoholism that's all too often true of the Establishment.

I called the policeman back and told him to come the following day. He said he'd be there by noon.

It was paramount that the children not find out what was to happen. Fortunately, the next day dawned hot and sunny, and I sent them off to the club, saying they were to stay all day and in no circumstances come home until late afternoon, as Daddy was very sick. I trusted them to mind me, and as an added inducement, once again—as I had before our first abortive attempt to run away—I told them to charge lunch. The thought of ordering a large spaghetti and pie à la mode immediately cemented the deal.

At eleven my doctor friends came over. "Let's have a look at you," Jim said to Sean, pulling out his stethoscope. "You're in pretty bad shape, old boy." And his wife said gently, "You really ought to be in a hospital, where you'd get the proper care. That's what hospitals are for—to help people get better." Sean was deeply fond of them and seemed to enjoy the attention. Like a sick child trying to be brave and independent, he took a swig from his bottle and smiled, saying, "Never a hospital—never, never." They went downstairs, signed the papers and left.

At noon the policeman called to say he would be an hour

late. In an effort to calm my nerves I set about defrosting the refrigerator, hammering off large chunks of ice with a cooking mallet. Halfway through the project I decided there was still one last out, and I went upstairs to my husband. I told him that he had to go to a hospital and had to go right now, to get dressed immediately and I'd drive him to the drying-out place for four days.

"I'm not going to any hospital, now or ever," he said wearily.

"Darling, if you don't come with me right now, I can assure you you're going to be in a hospital by five this evening. We can't go on like this," I said, unable to resist warning him.

"Don't try anything or you'll be dead by five this evening," he answered. And with that he got up, picked up his hatchet and made his way downstairs to the kitchen, where he stuffed his pockets with steak knives and then went into the living room and stretched out on the couch. Hoping he would be good and drunk when the policemen arrived, I put his bottle beside him. "I don't want that. Take it away," he mumbled.

At 1:30 p.m. the policeman called to say he would be unavoidably detained for another hour. I went to the upstairs phone and quietly called the local doctor I respected, told him what I was doing and asked him to come and give my husband a tranquilizing shot so that he would be asleep when it was time to leave.

When he arrived, Sean was lying on his back, breathing heavily, a shiny trickle of blood coming from his nose and running down the black stubble of beard, his distended stomach straining over his faded bathing trunks that hung in folds around his thin legs.

"This will make you feel better," the doctor said, administering the shot. My husband nodded weakly.

I walked out with the doctor to his car. "I'm trying to help him," I said, seeking if not his approval at least his forgiveness. "I know," he said gently. "Good luck." Then I went upstairs and cried, wishing I could hide forever and never have to face what

I was doing; but the clock said it was 2:15, so I made myself stop, washed my face and put on a linen dress and sandals, my commitment costume.

When I went downstairs Sean was asleep, and after carefully removing the knives and hatchet, I sat down with my back to him, looking out of the windows, waiting for the policeman's arrival. Finally I saw Jim and two tall burly men walking across the lawn. I went out to meet them, a loving wife turned ruthless conspirator. One of the men asked if he could bring his car, a police car, to the side door that opened onto the living room. As we waited for him, Jim told me he had called the state hospital and spoken to the admitting physician and arranged to have Sean given immediate attention. "But you've got to arrive before he goes off duty at four. And one other thing," he continued gravely. "Sometimes we have to do an act that seems very wrong at the time, but we do it in order to achieve something we believe is right. I want you to remember that and also I want you to see as little of this as possible. As soon as we go inside, you go upstairs and stay there until Sean is in the car."

We four went inside quietly and looked at the supine figure. The policeman broke the silence: "You'd better get him a soft shirt. The camisole is canvas, might be rough on his skin."

Sean sat bolt upright. "Get away from me," he said through clenched teeth. "Get away or you'll all be dead." I ran upstairs as my husband kicked the coffee table over and crouched behind it. When I came back with the shirt one policeman had twisted Sean's arm behind his back while the other one held out the bulky strait jacket. I ran back upstairs, my fist in my mouth to keep from screaming. There was shouting and scuffling and then I heard the car door slam. It was done.

I went downstairs and out to our car, ready to follow the policemen to the hospital. As I got in I saw one of the children's friends, standing by his bicycle, transfixed by the scene he had just witnessed.

Jim, who was ashen, came to my car. "Are you sure you don't want me to go with you?" he asked. "No," I answered, determined to do my own dirty work, "just take care of the children." He nodded, and I drove behind the police car. I could see the back of Sean's head. He was slumped to one side, a pig trussed for market; the policeman had asked me earlier if I wanted to ride along with them, in the same car, a farmerette bringing her prize to slaughter.

To my horror the lead car turned toward the village and went straight down Main Street, and then on to the town jail. I was too unnerved to protest and could only silently curse the policeman for not telling me this was part of the deal. Apparently he saw no difference between an alcoholic and a criminal. A manacled man was brought out and put in the back of the car with my husband. We started off again, retracing our route down Main Street, which led onto the highway.

The blistering August sun was directly in my eyes, and it took all my concentration to follow the speeding car ahead. I was afraid of losing it, as I didn't know where the hospital was, but in an hour we were there, driving through high wrought-iron gates into spacious grounds with clean rolling lawns and trees, heading toward a new-looking large red brick building identified by a sign reading "Hospital." It looked decent and I was relieved. But instead of stopping, we drove on by it and over the rise of a hill to a series of depressing old brownstone structures.

There had been no sign of human life in front of the hospital building, but here in front of a building labeled "Admissions" men were lying on the grass or milling around the entrance steps. The grounds were littered with paper cups, candy wrappers, and pop bottles. We drove on and turned into the courtyard of another building. All the windows were barred.

The police car parked near a door and, keeping my distance, I turned off the motor. I heard shouts, inarticulate but human sounds that echoed around the courtyard, and I looked up to see

141

arms reaching between the bars at the windows. Then I saw some laughing, chatting nurses come out of the building, the last one turning to lock the door behind her. It was four o'clock, and they were going off duty. This meant that the doctor who was to admit my alcoholic would no longer be available.

I honked my horn and beckoned to the policeman. "I've changed my mind," I said tersely, "I'm not leaving my husband here."

"Oh, don't worry," he answered calmly. "This is for the criminally insane. We're just dropping the other fellow off."

We then drove back, not to the red brick hospital but to the admissions building, where the men were loitering outside. We parked and the policeman strolled over to my car. "This is the admissions building," he explained. "We'll take him in now. Wanna come?"

"Is it necessary?" I asked, dreading to face Sean. He shrugged and then walked into the hospital. A character out of *Pal Joey*, traveling cap, striped tight jacket, black and white checked pants, strolled by and yelled to a nurse who was getting into her car, "Hey, sweetheart, I'm going to stick nails in all your tires and no one can do a fucking thing about it, 'cause I'm a nut!" He let out a whoop of laughter and headed into the building. For a minute his little joke helped.

The policeman reappeared with an attendant, who got inside the car and after a few seconds backed out, talked to the policeman and returned to the building. The policeman came to my car and told me the attendant said my husband was in such bad shape that he'd have to be taken directly to the hospital, the new red brick building, and that I was to stay behind to give my commitment papers to the admitting office.

"How bad is he?" I asked.

"He didn't say, ma'm, but his nose is bleeding a lot," he answered.

"How is he otherwise?" I asked numbly.

"He's okay," he answered amiably, "didn't cause trouble. Once he asked where we were taking him, and then he said the camisole was hurting his arm, so we loosened it up." He went back to his car and drove my husband away. I heard a clock chime five and went inside the admissions building.

A few sad, still people were sitting on benches in the immediate foyer, and beyond that there was a large, drab open hall, deserted except for a nurse at the information desk. I asked to see the doctor Jim had contacted, hoping that perhaps he had waited for us.

"He went off duty at four. Wait your turn with those others," she snapped.

"Will I have to wait long?" I asked, somehow confusing this place with Doctors Hospital in New York City.

"Your turn'll come," she answered, dismissing me.

I sat down on one of the benches and watched the clock tick on to 5:30. The whole ghastly business was taking much longer than I had anticipated; I hoped my friends were feeding the children.

At a quarter to six I got up and knocked on a door that said "Doctor." A thin, sallow-faced man opened it, and after introducing myself I said I had to get home to take care of my children. "I'll see you in a few minutes," he said softly with a slight accent, and then closed the door.

Finally he opened the door and motioned for me to come into his dingy, anonymous little office. The walls were bare, devoid of any degrees. He introduced himself, mentioning, in a sad voice, a French-sounding name.

"Now," he said, "tell me about your husband."

I desperately wanted him to understand that Sean was not just a drunken bum, and I told him, fighting back tears, that my husband was extremely bright, a lawyer, a wonderful husband and father, a man who had somehow become an alcoholic. I recited his medical history—Bellevue, the liver failure—and explained

143

again that being an extremely intelligent man, he would try to talk his way out of the hospital as soon as he was sober but that it was important that he stay for the full sixty days so that with psychiatric care he would have a chance to recover.

He looked at me with his dark, soulful eyes and said softly that the hospital would try to take care of him and for me to sign the commitment papers. I signed, and then he said I could go see my husband. (Why, I wondered, did anyone think I had the courage to see my husband? He wasn't my child or a friend; he was the man I loved, and I had plotted against him, trussed him up in a strait jacket and had him carted off to be institutionalized.)

I thanked him and said goodbye. Getting in the car, I decided it was best to stop by the hospital, if not to see Sean, at least to see the head doctor so that he could better understand the patient. Arriving at the red brick building, I found, to my great relief, that the interior was modern and clean. I told the nurse at the reception desk that I wanted to see the doctor who had examined my husband.

"Oh, he hasn't come in yet." She smiled. "There's no doctor on duty after four. We call one in for new admissions. He'll be here soon."

I waited, wondering if Sean was locked in a padded cell or strapped down to a bed. After fifteen or twenty minutes a little round Japanese man strode briskly to the elevator, and after another twenty minutes the nurse's phone rang. She said the doctor was ready to see me.

Leaving the elevator, I found myself in a deserted, brightly lighted hall. I turned a corner and saw a glass-enclosed office where the Japanese man sat at a desk.

"Ah, yes," he sibilated, smiling, "you're the wife of our new patient. Well, we've given your husband something to clot the blood, and we're feeding him intravenously, and we've given him something to make him sleep. In a few days he'll feel much better," he said cheerfully, and then added cordially. "But you can see for yourself. I will take you to him."

"No, I don't want to see him," I said, knowing that if I did I would go to pieces.

"You don't?" he asked with surprise. "Ah, well, yes, you look tired. Another time."

My head had begun to ache, and I asked if I could have an aspirin. He nodded and called for an orderly, to whom he handed a ring of keys.

"Of course, we keep all medication locked up," he explained, smiling. Again I thought it was necessary that he understand that Sean was not just a drunk and repeated what I had told the admitting doctor. The Japanese man kept nodding sympathetically. I asked if I could call in the morning to find out how my husband was doing.

"Ah, yes, call . . . call anytime you like," he assured me.

I thanked him and left. Waiting for the elevator, I could hear the collective breathing of the patients. The hall clock said 7:15, and they were all in bed.

As I drove out through the hospital gates I told myself that I had done the right thing, that the hospital was not half bad, and that when he was better Sean would understand and forgive me. I hadn't eaten all day and I felt giddy, almost elated. The longest day of my life was coming to an end.

It was after nine when I arrived home. The children wanted to know where I had been all day and what had happened to Daddy. I told them I had taken him to the hospital, where he would get the right care. Nicholas, the ten-year-old, asked if that meant Daddy was going to get well.

For the next few days I was somewhat in a state of shock, sometimes feeling that my husband was dead and other times that he was still lying in the darkened bedroom, and I'd go back upstairs to prove to myself that he was gone. Then, gradually, I began to relax and the house began to seem a pleasant place to live. Miraculously, I had not had to run away. We were home and could look forward to sixty days of peace.

My daily calls to the hospital yielded nothing more than a

perfunctory "satisfactory condition" report, as I could never get through to a doctor. There were only two visiting days a week, and on the first one, a Sunday, four days after Sean had been admitted, I set off at nine in the morning to visit him.

I felt perfectly calm during the drive, but going up in the elevator, I took a deep breath, anticipating recriminations. An attendant told me to wait in the visitors room, and on my way I passed a roomful of hollow-eyed old men, sitting motionless in wheelchairs, lonely, gaunt figures all staring at the cartoon figures skittering across the television set. Then I saw Sean, leaning on the arm of a nurse, walking very slowly down the hall. He was wearing a robe, pajamas and slippers, and he was clean-shaven and his hair was combed; and he was smiling, ever so slightly, his sweet crooked grin. He had forgiven me. I put my arms around the man I adored and wanted to save, and I tried not to cry as I told him how marvelous he looked.

He nodded and smiled as I showed him his presents and told him about the children. After he had gotten his breath, he said we'd talk about that later, but right now I had to promise to take him home with me today. He was so nervous he was almost in tears as he told me that if he weren't already crazy he would certainly become so if he stayed there another day, that the place was filthy, the food abominable, that he couldn't sleep because people babbled in their sleep all night and the attendants spent the night screwing each other, that they wouldn't even allow him to shave himself, that he had had to beg to be allowed to shower, and that the second day he was there he had been given tests which included questions on the Constitution, which he had answered 100 percent correctly, even though they kept him doped up.

"You've got to get me out of here," he said, looking into my eyes, "and I promise you that I will never—never ever in my life —take another drink. This place is full of crazy people, real nuts."

I told him there was nothing I could do because it was

Sunday and there was no doctor on duty but that I would look into the matter early in the week.

When I returned home I told Jim about the way Sean felt toward the hospital. He said he could understand Sean's antipathy to the state hospital and had an alternate plan in mind for him. He had compiled a list of private hospitals and retreats that dealt in depth with alcoholism, from fifty dollars a week upward, and he recommended that I make my husband's release contingent on his signing himself into one of these programs. I was delighted with Jim's idea; it was a way to make sure that Sean received help but took him out of the demeaning situation of the mental hospital, with all those "nuts."

Knowing he would use the depleted state of our finances as an excuse not to pay to go anywhere, I decided to swallow my pride once again and ask for financial help. When I was in Florida I had been told that members of one of his former law firms had discussed the matter of paying for his hospitalization at an expensive sanitarium that specialized in the treatment of alcoholics. I went back to the partner with whom I had discussed commitment and explained the plan, asking if he would reopen the retreat matter. I told him I didn't think the firm owed either myself or my husband anything, but I didn't know where else to turn for several thousand dollars and if Sean didn't have a better and longer chance to recover, hopes for his future were very dim. He agreed to look into the possibility.

I never heard from him again, but it didn't matter. A week later Sean called to tell me he was being released. He had petitioned the administration to release him after fourteen days so that he could volunteer for the hospital's special six-week program for alcoholics. The petition had been accepted. I must not have read the fine print in my commitment papers carefully enough. Instead of lasting over eight weeks, his commitment had lasted exactly two.

On the day he was to be signed out and into the voluntary

147

program I drove to the admissions building, where he was now housed, and when I arrived and saw him sitting on a rail fence, wearing the baggy, nondescript clothes he had been issued, he looked exactly like all the other patients lolling about. We went inside to await the transfer papers, sitting in the large drab visitors lounge, eating the lunch I had brought. He was telling me about the program, said to be an outstanding one for a state hospital, when one of the patients, standing in a long line going into the lunchroom, suddenly started to scream. Two orderlies rushed toward him and hustled him off down the corridor, still screaming frightening, choking sounds. Sean and I looked at each other. He put his hand over mine and gave it a squeeze. How in God's name, I wondered, had the two of us found our way to a place like this?

Finally it was time for the transfer. The pale, aesthetic-looking psychiatrist with whom I had had the original interview came to say goodbye. Sean greeted him almost with affection, and the doctor responded in kind. As we walked to the main entrance he said in his soft, accented voice, "I have had many talks with your husband. He is a very sick man, but if he can learn to live without alcohol he can lead a full, good life. The program he is entering is not fancy, the accommodations are very simple, but the program itself is as good as he can get anywhere. Take care of yourself," he said, putting his arm around my husband's shoulders. "Your liver is badly damaged . . . and good luck."

I decided he was a good man, limited by the enormity of his work, with too many sick people to attend and neither the time nor the facilities to treat them properly.

It was a hospital rule that patients had to be transferred to new quarters by a medical attendant, so my husband went off with a nurse in her car and I followed in mine. The grounds were rather beautiful, like a large park, with sturdy old oaks and elms and occasional low brownstone buildings that looked as if they might have once been stables. We passed a group of children, walking two by two and flanked by several nurses, and then, around the bend in the winding road, came to a large building identified as being for children who were mental patients.

Thank God our own are sound, I thought automatically.

We stopped in front of a dark brick two-story building with a long front porch that had several rocking chairs on it. It looked a lonely place, but peaceful. Across the road was a severe-looking four-story building that reminded me of a stark, rundown old New England factory. There were men lying on the grounds, seemingly asleep, more Rip Van Winkles, dozing away their lives in the middle of the day. Sean later told me these were the alcoholics who had been committed for long periods, some for life, the ones whose brains had been affected, near vegetables, kept alive and kept tranquilized. ("Alcoholism is a progressive disease . . . which has only two outlets: insanity or death.")

The transfer nurse said she would take my husband in to register and then return him to me so that we could have a chance to talk. Sean had told me briefly a few of the grisly details of life in the admissions building, a crowded catch-all for new patients who had every kind of mental illness that he said made the red brick hospital seem like a luxury resort by comparison. For the past week he had been sleeping in a dorm full of men who, night and day, screamed or muttered or masturbated or sat on the floor, staring silently into space, and having set the scene, neither of us wanted to talk about it anymore. I had told him of our activities at home and of course that I loved him, believed in him and was proud of him for making this decision; but I couldn't go on in that vein without sounding like a Pollyanna.

I sat down on a park bench and watched a man in the distance as he hit a golf ball toward a particular tree, after which he walked the hundred yards to the tree and hit the ball back to the original spot—back and forth, back and forth, always accurately. Sean later told me this was what the man did all day, every day.

My husband gave me a cheerful wave as he came out of the building.

"It's not exactly great," he said wryly, "but it's a definite improvement over my former lodgings."

We ate the rest of the grapes from the picnic and chatted as best we could until it was after three, and then I said I had to go home to fix the children's supper.

"Why are you always running away from me?" Sean asked accusingly.

"I'm not running away," I said. "I just can't be in two places at the same time, and someone has to take care of the boys." But he had spoken the bitter truth, and driving away I was glad, in a guilty way, to be leaving such a depressing place.

∾ 11 ∾

A Matter of Morality?

That was on Tuesday, and the following Thursday night Sean called to say he was allowed a weekend pass and to pick him up on Friday at noon.

"Do you think you're ready to come home?" I asked, stunned.

Instead of answering my question, he told me that the program operated on an honor system and that he had to be back on Sunday night by six but that he would somehow arrange his transportation back so that I wouldn't have to drive him there.

I couldn't believe my ears. I had told the psychiatrist of his four-year history of alcoholism; I had brought him into the state hospital a mental and physical wreck for a sixty-day period, from which he had been released after fourteen days; and now, after only three days in the hospital's voluntary rehabilitation program, it was assumed that he was capable of leaving for a weekend at home, as free as anyone else to get a drink.

I called the program supervisor and asked if it was true that my husband was to be given the weekend off.

"Yes," he said. "We feel these short trips home give our men confidence in their ability to control the problem. Of course, if they take a single drink, they can't come back. It's the honor system."

"But I don't think my husband is ready for that yet," I protested. "How could he be?"

"We have to let the men themselves make that decision," he said.

To all intents and purposes, the city hall of the volunteer program had made an alliance with my husband, and it was futile trying to fight both of them. He wanted out, and the control was perfectly willing to let him out, the only stipulation being that he not take a drink; and if he did, then he was to own up to it and retire from the program. I was deeply puzzled. What did an "honor system" have to do, therapeutically, with a sick person or addict? This kind of honor system was based on the assumption that alcoholics were capable of controlling their drinking; they could stop or not stop, and if they preferred not to stop they must be manly enough to admit it and gracefully retire from the program and once again be free to pursue their addiction. In effect it treated alcoholism as a matter of morality and will power—a question of the survival of the fittest—rather than as a disease.

The first weekend was challenging. Sean was terribly nervous and it made everyone else nervous, which made him more nervous, etc., and I wondered how this was supposed to buttress the honor system rather than creating ideal conditions not just for wanting a drink but needing one. However, he passed the test. There was no liquor in the house, and I plied him with hearty meals. He was ravenous and said that the food in the program was so poor, so tasteless, that everyone carried a container of hot peppers to put on everything, no matter what the meal, breakfast, lunch, or dinner.

But the next weekend he flunked the honor system. He answered the phone when someone called, inviting us for cocktails. (Only my closest friends knew of the commitment.) I said no, it was too soon, but Sean insisted on going whether I went or not. I relented, in order to play bird dog, on the condition that we have dinner first, hoping that a full meal would lessen his appetite for a drink. We were hardly in the door when the waiter asked our preference. "Tonic with a slice of lemon," said I. "Scotch and soda," said he. Remarkably, he had only two drinks and dutifully returned to the program the following evening. It never occurred to me to tell control he had broken the number-one rule. The handwriting was on the wall, but I wanted him to have another chance. And I wanted the full time off, free of the strain of his presence, before he returned.

But the full time turned out to be two-thirds time. Sean deducted the two weeks he had spent in the hospital and admissions building from the six-week volunteer period, and four weeks after he had entered his rehabilitation program he called to tell me that he had completed the course and to come and pick him up. Brushing aside my suggestion that two more weeks there might be wise, he announced that it was vital that he return to work and start making money and that he fully understood what he considered to be the only meaningful lesson—i.e., it takes only one drink to change one's judgment, ergo never take the first drink. He said the constant doses of AA *mea culpa* philosophy, the confession sessions—the priest who drank the sacramental wine, the man whose son had drowned because the father left the beach to sneak a drink in his car—didn't relate to his own life.

When I went to pick him up I met the head of the state hospital's AA program, a pleasant man in his fifties. He told me about AA precepts and pointed with pride to the posters his boys had made. They were meant to be humorous, pointing to the pitfalls of a single glass of beer, with one showing the classic drunk supporting a lamppost, the kind of wit and art one sees in a high-school yearbook. I voiced my admiration, all the while think-ing, This is hardly the kind of message that is going to score with Sean.

As we left the AA man put his arm around my husband and told me that he was a good man and I should take care of him. Shaking hands, he said to Sean, "Now the second—no, the sec-ond before—you think you want a drink, call on us. That's what we're here for, and we're the ones who can understand you best." He was a well-meaning man, anxious to help; but the best he could offer was the buddy system, moral support rather than therapy.

I had forgotten to bring my husband's driver's license, and this immediately made him angry. He asked, bitterly, if I thought he was mentally incompetent to drive and then proceeded to criticize my every move, shifting, braking, accelerating, passing, whatever. Although I wanted with all my heart to make his return a success, to ease his resentment, I felt myself growing hostile, and by the time we reached the village we were barely speaking. He told me to stop the car so he could walk home and work off his tension. When he arrived at our house, two hours later, he was carrying the familiar brown paper bag. He went straight up to bed with his bottle. I called the psychiatrist at the volunteer program. She was very cordial, and to prove her expertise she blandly told me that she had known all along that he wasn't "quite" ready to admit and accept his alcoholism.

What had been the point in trussing him up in a strait jacket, which, despite my well-meaning intentions, was a cal-culated, vicious act? And what about shipping him off to the state mental hospital? I decided the doctors who had refused to sign my papers were right, as right as my doctor friends who had urged his commitment. And conversely, they were—as a group—all wrong, being on opposite sides but equidistant from the plumb line of an unworkable situation. It was inhumane not to try to help my alcoholic, but within the system, or lack thereof, it was useless to try.

That was the only time I ever committed him. During the next two years he went back to the state hospital twice, but I had nothing to do with the formalities, neither getting the papers signed nor hiring his transportation. The local police and the county medical officer made all the arrangements, and I have no idea, only a chilling suspicion, whether he was carted off in a camisole or in handcuffs in the back of a paddy wagon.

Nor did I ever visit him there again, because by the time it happened next I myself had "hit the bottom," and the only way I could claw my way back up was to turn my back on the one I most wanted to help. Alcoholism literature errs in limiting the bottom to the drinker; there is a similar area, again relative and undefined, for the alcoholic's mate. This bottom is a land of abject despair, and getting out means giving up.

❧ 12 ❧

A Hopeless Life
Winter 1967–1968

As a family we were now at the point of no return, literally and figuratively. Returning to New York, finding another apartment, putting the children in private schools, all this was financially impossible; and for me, seeking a legal separation or running away again was also out and for the same reason: no money. And searching for a medical remedy was obviously futile. So, with a kind of Zen calm, I accepted our fate of drifting or plummeting on downward to the bottom. Next stop, the poor house, but in the meantime we had a roof over our heads, and I had neither the strength nor the vision to ask for anything more.

I enrolled the children in the East Hampton public schools and, as there was no heat in our house, rented another for the winter. It belonged to casual friends, both of whom were doctors who knew of my husband's alcoholism and also were perfectly aware that we had four sons, similar in ages to their own three boys. It was a nice little house, decorated in contemporary *Good*

Housekeeping style, hidden away on a wooded lane near a large pond, a summer-people area, isolated in the winter. It was really too small for a family of six, and we were always all together in the living room, but it was very reasonable; the doctors were anxious to have their house heated during the winter and at someone else's expense. I carefully packed away their bibelots and removed all other fragile or damagable items, and we settled in to wait for what was to come. And it came, in wave after wave of unyielding sadness and madness.

Early in the fall Sean finally got arrested for drunken driving. (Amazingly, it was the first time.) The police called me, and I went to the jail to see him, ignoring his enraged demands that I get him a drink, and later to court to bail him out, looking straight ahead as he told the judge I was a bitch and therefore the police must take him home, as he could not bear to ride with me. When the local bar called in the middle of the day to ask me to come and get my husband (the bartender was willing to sell him drinks but not to have a drunk on the premises) I'd numbly drive to the bar, ask for assistance in getting Sean out to the car, self-consciously ignoring the onlookers; or, if the police brought my husband home (in lieu of locking him up for public intoxication), I sedately thanked them for their courtesy. And when my alcoholic ranted and raved that I was ruining his life and, to prove the point, knocked the furniture about, I'd quietly sit and listen and then put everything back in place. It made it difficult for the children to do homework and impossible for them to bring new friends home from school, but I explained that Daddy was desperately sick. I didn't know what else to say to them.

Similarly, I knew we were running out of money, but I didn't know what to do about it. We owed insurance premiums, back rent on the house, the utilities, telephone, drugstore, almost everyone in town except the liquor store. When my husband said we must cash in the eight thousand in stocks he had given me (until then safely resting in his safety-deposit box), as his securities were now gone, I agreed, even to the extent of depositing the money in his bank account. I then sat down and wrote out checks for half that amount (he was in no condition to do anything but sign), and I neither knew nor cared what was to happen when the rest was gone. I could have used the money to run away again, but I didn't have the strength to pull the children out of school once more and set off for God knows where; nor did I have the heart. Doctors had assured me my alcoholic was going to die, and it was immobilizing to watch him deteriorate.

At times he appeared catatonic, sitting for long periods, absolutely still, arms folded across his chest, no expression on his face, his eyes always hidden by dark glasses. Occasionally a tear rolled down one cheek. When he was like this, or when he spent days in bed, barely breathing, his face twisting in pain, I could only cry.

The saddest times of all, evoking pale shadows of our former life, were the days when he was sober. We would walk together on the deserted winter beach, Sean moving like an old tired man, pausing to get his breath after a short distance. Or we'd all go skating on the nearby pond, the black ice slick and smooth, but now instead of leading the boys in ice hockey or teaching them to skate backward, he maneuvered cautiously, intent on not falling, crouched in fear like a tentative novice. Sometimes we'd sit by the fire, talking about the antics of the dog or the wonders of our children, always speaking of the past or the present but never making future plans. The future didn't exist.

I knew I was sinking into depression, and at first I tried to buck myself up by going into the city for a night to see friends and take my mind off my troubles. On my second attempt, in the midst of a pleasant little dinner party, I received a call from an East Hampton summer friend who was English, very sophisticated, even a bit brittle but straightforward; I liked her. I was surprised and delighted to hear her voice. But she hadn't called to chat.

159

"Thank God I've found you," she began in an anguished tone. "Listen, my dear, the most awful thing happened today. We'd spent the weekend in the country, and Sean called and asked if we'd give him a lift into the city today, and naturally we said yes. He sounded fine at the time, and then when we went to pick him up this afternoon he came crawling—and I mean literally crawling, on his hands and knees—out to the car. He couldn't even stand. And there were those darling sons of yours standing there saying they could take care of him and it was all right, but of course it wasn't all right. It was ghastly. Walter helped them get him inside. My God, he was an absolute dead weight. I mean he couldn't move—and I felt awful leaving those children in a situation like that, but Walter had to be back in town for business and the boys said they'd be fine, but, oh my God, it's so tragic. Sean's such a decent man, really. I kept saying to myself, 'What if it were Walter? What if it were Walter?' I don't know what I'd do."

That was my last trip to the city. The children were my responsibility, and it was my duty to stay with them, to try to make their lives easier, even if it meant constantly living in isolation with my alcoholic. Having always been a summer person, I knew no one in the year-round population. My only friend was the bottle. As long as the children were up I limited myself to two drinks before dinner; but once they were on their way to bed I felt I owed myself a cup of comfort to compensate for the weary life. I'd have a drink about nine and then another and then another or so. And the alcohol, combined with loneliness and the strain and pain of our life, packed quite a wallop. Without realizing it, I was turning a bit mad myself.

My aberrations weren't serious so long as my alcoholic was quiet. At those times I would merely get quietly ossified, reading I knew not what or staring into space, musing about the sadness of life. However, after spending the day immobilized, he often came on at night like Lazarus and would persist in talking to me, whether I was trying to read or, later, sleep, endlessly fantasizing about the "Russkies" and "Krauts" who were after him until the early-morning hours. However, instead of listening to his fantasies, I began to engage in my own. Stimulated or lulled, as the case may be, by my drinks, I'd silently mull over the possibilities of killing my alcoholic. In many ways it seemed the only solution.

I thought of closing the doors and windows and turning on the gas while the children were at school; but this was too simple, as Sean had a very keen sense of smell and, furthermore, we were living in a rented house and I didn't know if the gas might cause it to blow up, which I certainly didn't want to happen. I thought of driving him, when he was passed out in the car, to a cliff at Montauk that dropped a hundred feet into the sea and somehow pushing the car over the side while I myself escaped; but I knew I'd flub this, as there is none of the daredevil in me. I wondered what would happen if I poured ammonia or clorox into his gin. As I finally had gotten rid of his rifle, the only way to kill him with weapons was to stab him, and I'd lie in bed at night and wonder if I had the courage to take a kitchen knife and push the blade into his heart. Would his flesh respond like a side of beef? Would he open his eyes and look at me before he died, or would he, with his ability to second-guess me, grab the knife and kill me instead?

Even if I succeeded, could the children stand the strain of my trial and subsequent imprisonment? When I was fortified with drink, the thought of prison life didn't seem much worse than my present one, and I knew I would be convicted. The fact that my husband's alcoholism was driving us both mad and was having a disastrous impact on the children would be of no consequence, even though there was no other remedy, legally or medically.

Fantasies such as these marked the extent of my positive thinking, and the next morning I'd tell myself that I had to stop drinking at night. But by evening my resolve had weakened.

The doctors said my alcoholic was going to die if he didn't

stop drinking, but he didn't stop drinking, and as the winter wore on he didn't die. We were quite clearly and inevitably running out of money, and though we could sell the house, Sean refused to do so, and I couldn't because it was in his name. And soon we wouldn't be able to pay his insurance premiums, which meant that when he finally did die, $85,000 would have gone down the drain.

The winter wore on into spring. Robert Kennedy and Martin Luther King were assassinated, but my alcoholic kept on living and drinking, now lying in front of the television set, constantly tuned into the endless funeral coverage. I rarely watched. Living in isolation with this strange, confused man who had once been my husband made the senseless, tragic murders seem only another extension of our own locked-in, lunatic world.

And so, without personally landing in jail or on Skid Row, I, like the proverbial alcoholic, had "hit the bottom." It was a position of total despair. I saw no way out. Everything I had tried had failed, and the only constant in our lives was my alcoholic. And he was mine, all mine, too sick and helpless to be cast aside, yet not sick enough to be treated. He had become a nonentity, the forgotten man, a drunk, and no one wanted any part of him, neither his family (his brothers and sister) nor his friends, nor even, as I was to learn, the United States Government.

A friend of mine who did tax work told me that Sean could collect Social Security on the basis of being incapacitated, not by alcoholism but by his cirrhosis, and with four children and a wife, this could mean a monthly check in the neighborhood of three hundred dollars. From time to time during the winter he had gone into New York in a useless and pathetic attempt to look for a job and, on occasion, had gone to Dr. Pierce, the New York doctor who had refused to treat him for alcoholism but continued to treat him for its related manifestations—gastrointestinal disorders, skin infections, wounds caused by falls. I wrote Dr. Pierce and asked for a letter stating that my husband had cirrhosis, and he sent one to me. It was addressed to To Whom It May Concern, and it stated that his patient had been in his office on "May 3rd of this year, suffering from Laennec's cirrhosis of the liver with ascites. Because of this illness he is disabled and unable to work."

I drove fifty miles to the nearest Social Security office and presented my letter to one of the agents, who read it and said, yes, my husband was certainly entitled to Social Security payments and that I was to bring him in for an examination, as his condition had to be verified by agency doctors.

I told the agent that I couldn't bring my husband in, that he was bedridden and, moreover, that he opposed the idea on the basis that it was a form of welfare.

"Social Security is not welfare," he said. "Your husband has worked a good many years, and he's entitled to his Social Security on the grounds of disability. Tell your husband that and I'm sure he'll understand and come here to the office for an examination."

I sadly explained that, in addition to having cirrhosis, my husband was also an alcoholic and, as such, was usually under the influence of alcohol and therefore not reasonable; and further that it wasn't a question as to whether or not he, in his befogged mind, thought he should collect Social Security but rather that, since he couldn't work and had no income, we, his family, needed the money.

"Don't you have field doctors who could come to our house and examine him?" I asked.

"Well, yes, we do," he said, "but you must understand that they have many, many sick people to see—men and women who are really sick and can't leave their homes. We schedule these visits months in advance and only for people who are really seriously ill, incapacitated."

I explained again that my husband was also very seriously ill, as the letter from the doctor said; he could not work, we had no income, and therefore he was entitled to Social Security payments.

"Now, what difference does it make if he can't or won't

come to this office? If he's entitled to Social Security, why is he not also entitled to the services of a field doctor?"

"Can't you get your husband to AA?" the agent answered judiciously, and I knew I was working on a lost cause. I left, went home and reported to Sean what had happened. He would have none of it.

Dr. Pierce's salutation—To Whom It May Concern—was a joke. My husband's cirrhosis, his alcoholism, concerned nobody but me. Our situation was desperate, too desperate to ignore, and yet in my slough of despair I couldn't think of what to do or where to turn next.

Having joined the Catholic Church because I was so happy with my life, I now clung to it because I was so miserable, and I regularly went to Mass, seeking its soothing order and dignity and peace. I believed that God would somehow help me to find a way out of the mess we had made of our lives.

One Sunday late in the spring I was gazing at the altar, transfixed by depression rather than adoration. In my heart I still wanted to do the right thing by my alcoholic; I believed in love, but the long sad winter of desolation was a cross heavier than I could bear. It had weighted me down, down to the bottom where life no longer held a single strand of joy. Wonderful friends had tried to make my life more pleasant—long-distance calls, an occasional gift, sometimes a self-conscious visit—but there was no way they could wash out the sorry scene. I was tired of having people feeling sorry for me, and I was tired of feeling sorry for Sean and the children and for myself.

Suddenly, almost as if God had spoken to me, I felt a surge of resolve, a regeneration of energy. I wasn't a mystic, but I had the definite feeling that I had new strength to take a flight to action, to escape the slough for a more positive life and to do it with God's blessing.

The first step was to go to New York and look for a job. I recalled my trip the previous fall when my friend had called and told me about Sean crawling to the car on his hands and knees, and I remembered how guilty I had felt about the children; but as I sat in church, leaving them no longer loomed as an overwhelming problem. I decided that the boys could manage and that it was more important that I try to pull myself together. By the end of the Mass I felt quite elated. I wasn't made of the stuff of martyrs or saints, and I wanted out of our life. Now and at whatever cost.

Sean was angry when I told him of my job-hunting plan, but that didn't deter me, and the following morning I left for the city, armed with the classifieds from the *Times* and a portfolio crammed with proposals and press kits from my previous jobs. After the long isolation of the country, the hustle and bustle of the city made me feel even more exhilarated, and I confidently set off to make the rounds of employment agencies.

By midafternoon my confidence was running thin. I was repeatedly turned down on the grounds that I hadn't worked in New York in nearly two years and therefore my experience was obsolete, and with each turn-down my idea of working in New York began to seem more unrealistic. What would I really do about Sean and the children? I began to worry about leaving them overnight and decided to abandon the project and take the late-afternoon train home. Just before boarding I called a friend at a large public-relations office and asked her to call me if any freelance jobs came up. Ten days later she phoned to say her firm was looking for someone who could travel and talk to teen-age groups about parties, and since I had some teen-agers and must, therefore, know what made that age-group tick, would I like to discuss the matter with the account executive in charge of the project? The account executive then came on the phone, explaining that the assignment was unique in so far as the client, a snack-food concern, had not previously explored the teen market, and it would require a person with considerable insight into the manners and mores of that age group, as well as the ability to communicate with them on a creative level. He then asked what I thought my qualifications were for such an assignment.

As an observer of the teen party scene my qualifications were zero. The two oldest boys had reached that age after Sean had become an alcoholic, and it never occurred to them to have a party with a drunken Dad on the premises. But I wanted to take a crack at the job, so I said, "Well, I'm not afraid of teen-agers, if that's what you mean."

There were several seconds of silence, then he laughed and said he guessed that was exactly what he meant, and we made an appointment for the following week.

Manny was a gracious, bolstering man who immediately made me feel special and competent, and after a short chat he announced that I was exactly the right person to carry his client's message to the younger generation. For the initial three-day in-store party clinic, plus time spent traveling, thinking, planning and meeting to discuss the project, I would receive seventy-five dollars a day, plus expenses. When I heard him say this I almost fell off my chair, awe-struck again that one never knows when a sudden shaft of light will pierce the gloom.

The effect on my morale was immediate. At home I now had something to think about other than our dreary daily life, and there was the added fillip of paid trips into town for meetings, with expense-account luncheons in expensive restaurants. The children were impressed by my earning powers, fancied the idea of my being involved with teen-agers and snacks (the company, Wise, made their favorite brand) and joined me in thinking up ideas for mythical parties. They said they didn't mind if I had to be away. I bought some new make-up for my personal appearances, and that made me feel good, too, especially as Manny said to put such necessities on my expense account.

My three-day party clinic turned out to be a success, and shortly thereafter I was sent on a three-day trip through New England, appearing on radio and TV, being interviewed by the local press, always describing the fun and games my teen-agers arranged for their own parties at home and giving advice on how to raise young people so that they became conscientious and cordial young teens. I enjoyed the job, but physically it was hard work, driving from city to city, always on the verge of getting lost and not finding an out-of-the-way radio station in time for my scheduled appearance, loaded down with my props, which included several six-foot-long loaves of bread and a helium tank for the balloons I recommended for decorations (I had one batch stamped with "Help Stamp Out Reality," a current teen slogan and one with which I could readily identify), changing clothes and make-up en route, and piling into motels at night dead beat, a regular Mrs. Willy Loman. But it was a stimulating change and the promotion received good coverage, and my pay was raised to eighty-five a day with plans for additional trips over the summer.

13

Giving Up
Summer 1968

The lease was up on our rented house, and we moved back into our own. Without any heat and with frequent fogs rolling in from the ocean, it was cold and damp and depressing. There was no money to repair cracked windows or clean dank slipcovers and rugs and no way short of a total paint job to stem the tide of mildew that crept across the walls. But the most depressing aspect of all was Sean, stretched out asleep or sitting mute in the living room, unshaven and unkempt, his eyes always hidden by dark glasses, a rigid and unreal pop-art figure of doom and gloom.

He had taken up a new kind of torment. As I was ironing or peeling vegetables, he'd silently appear behind me, whispering over and over, "Bitch . . . non-woman . . . bitch . . . bitch" and if I left my station, he'd follow, repeating the lines, a retarded child dogging my heels. (This was a man who had been admitted to argue before the Supreme Court of the United States.) To escape I spent my free daytime hours painting the small cottage on our property. In the past we had usually rented it during the summer, and though I knew this would be impossible as long as my madman was on the premises, it was a safe place to get away from him because the paint fumes made him gag. But at night there was no escape, and one evening, while the children sat with us in the living room trying to do their homework and I sat with a drink and the paper, trying to ignore his persistent whispered "Bitch . . . bitch," something snapped. I lunged at him, beating him on the head. He fought back, and while the two older boys tried to pull us apart, the door opened and in walked my sister Pat with her six children in tow. They had just arrived to spend the summer in their large house nearby.

Their arrival stopped the fight but not the furor. I asked my sister if I could stay at her house, and suddenly my alcoholic had a kitchen knife at my throat, saying I couldn't leave, and I yelled to one of the children to call the police. I heard the siren in a matter of minutes. Two policemen came inside, surrounded by the combined ten children. It was my chance to escape from our madhouse, and I could only speak in hyperbole: "My husband tried to kill me. He won't let me leave," I gasped.

"Are you over eighteen?" the officer asked pleasantly. I nodded. "Then you can leave the house anytime you want. Isn't that so, sir?" he said to Sean. "You're a lawyer, you must know that." And then, turning to me, he said, smiling, "Do you want to leave now?"

Again I nodded, and we all went out to my sister's station wagon. The roof light on the police car was flashing red through the dusk, casting a bizarre psychedelic light on the serene countryside as we drove off in silence. Pat and I had always been close, but it was hard to talk that evening. She was deeply fond of Sean, and all she could say was "You've got to do something" and all I could answer was "Yes. But what?" Sean was too sick to know what he was doing, and I knew there was more trouble in store.

The next morning I was in the kitchen sipping coffee and

talking to my fifteen- and sixteen-year-old nephews about their prep-school life. The oldest, whose speech was heavily larded with yes-sirs and no-sirs, was at the sink, which abutted on the wide windows. They were opened and had not yet been screened. I heard a car door slam and stood up to see a crazed man walking toward the windows. My alcoholic wasn't wearing his glasses, and his eyes were fixed in a glazed cold stare. He tried the kitchen door, which was locked, and then reached through the windows and picked up a carving knife as my nephew tried to slam the windows closed, saying, "Please, sir, you mustn't do that, sir. No, Uncle Sean, stop!"

My alcoholic picked up one of the screens that lay outside and began smashing the glass and frames. I called the police, and a few seconds later the same big officer of the night before strode up to the back porch. He wrestled the screen from my husband, somehow managing to pin his arms back, and handcuffed him. I ran upstairs to hide from the awful sight I had caused to happen.

Half an hour later the police chief called to say that my husband was in the lock-up, and if they were to hold him my sister would have to come down to the station and sign a complaint. I told him my husband was a very sick man and didn't belong in jail but should be sent to a hospital. The officer said that was not his area, and did my sister want to sign a complaint or didn't she? If not, my husband would be released.

"Can you hold him for a few hours, long enough to give me time to pack and leave? Then he can come home," I said. I felt guilty and preferred running away to having him sentenced to jail.

"That's up to you," the officer said.

I went home to pack and found my clothes, dresses, lingerie, shoes, purses, slashed and in tatters all over our bedroom and the picture of me in my wedding dress smashed. I was too dazed to care and left our room to pack up the boys' clothes. When I returned to my sister's to pick up the children, Pat said a psychiatrist had called and wanted to talk to me. I called, and the man, whom I did not know, told me that my husband was very sick, mentally and physically, and should be hospitalized.

"Do what you think is best," I said. "I'm leaving town." A short while later the police chief called to say that my husband had been committed to the state hospital for the usual sixty-day period. I knew that meant fourteen days, but it also meant I didn't have to run away that very day and would have two weeks to plan what my next move should be. It was a welcome reprieve, but I felt hollow and stunned, seeing in my mind's eye a montage of Sean smashing the windows, being handcuffed, sitting in a jail cell, lying in a hospital bed and being fed intravenously. For better or for worse, until death do us part; it was an anguishing price to pay for breaking out.

The next day I called a friend who had considerable political influence and asked him if there was any way he could assure my husband's commitment for the full sixty days. He was very sympathetic, and several days later I received a notice from the hospital saying that my husband's commitment had been extended to ninety days. Influence, like money, can be the instant magic ingredient.

I now had only two problems left: one, to make enough money to survive, and two, to get a legal separation, hopefully before my husband was released from the hospital so that he couldn't move back in with us.

Finances had to take priority. My total assets consisted of four hundred dollars saved from my teen-party work, and my financial responsibilities, in addition to feeding four children, paying utilities, phone, etc., included a four-hundred-dollar over-due tax bill, another three hundred dollars in life-insurance payments, and six hundred for club dues. As for the latter, I hoped that by never appearing at the club myself, the board of governors would ignore the children's presence so that they could continue to be with their friends and participate in the sports program. (Although it was supposed to be a very stuffy club, the board had been sympathetic to the extent of not asking us to resign when Sean's drinking warranted it and thus not heaping further embarrassment on the children.) I didn't want them to be at loose ends while I was out trying to earn money, yet there was simply no way to pay the bill.

The freshly painted cottage was readily rented for the season, and this brought in a thousand dollars. At the same time, a girl friend called to ask if I knew of a small house she could rent for two weeks, and I volunteered the downstairs part of mine, saying I would be away and the boys would be out most of the time. She agreed and wrote me a check for two hundred and fifty. I stocked up on groceries and then moved into the New York City apartment of friends who were away for the summer and set about tracking down free-lance jobs and also tracking down my lawyer again.

I had another lucky break when a friend asked if I would baby-sit his office during the same two weeks while his secretary was on vacation. I agreed, for one hundred and ten a week, on the condition that I could take time off to look for other jobs. The looking turned out to be very easy. I called Manny, and he introduced me to another account executive at his public-relations firm, and she gave me a writing assignment for one of her clients, a leading couture house.

The assignment was to write a position paper on the life style —dress, jewelry, make-up, etc.—of the "beautiful people." As I sat in my friend's office (he was a dealer in precious jewels, and he and his partner spent most of their day sitting in solitary splendor in the adjoining office, fondling their diamonds and pearls), working on my position paper, I mused that I was probably the most unqualified person in New York to be writing about "beautiful people." My husband was in the insane asylum, our house was falling to pieces, I had practically no clothes, was living rent free and trying to juggle two jobs at once to keep from going under. My dire position must have given me more objectivity and let my mind swing free, because the client was pleased and paid the five-hundred-dollar fee. And then, because the client couldn't decide what should be said on the subject of skirt lengths, I was paid another one hundred for a day's rewrite job. With the two thousand dollars I had garnered in the first two weeks of Sean's commitment I was able to pay the most pressing bills and maintain some kind of stability for the children. (I heard nothing from the club *vis-à-vis* the bill, and the boys continued to spend their days swimming and tennising. The consideration was gratifying.)

My legal problems were something else again.

In 1965 and again in 1967 I had sought a legal separation rather than a divorce because I thought of it basically as a holding operation, a period of time in which to program a more sane life for the children and myself while Sean hopefully worked out his drinking problems. It never occurred to me to seek a divorce; I hadn't even thought through the details of what was his and what was mine. I wanted the apartment in New York because it was home nine months of the year, rent-controlled and conveniently located. In so far as the East Hampton house was concerned, that was a summer place and in no way indispensable, especially after the summers there had started to become nightmarish. I had never once mentioned its disposition to my lawyer.

Now, however, four years after my first legal session, I still wanted a separation rather than a divorce, but for more calculated, less compassionate reasons: I wanted a legal separation so that I could claim that the East Hampton house, which was exclusively in Sean's name, was our only family domicile, and as such—since I would still be married to him even though legally separated—we could live there rent free for the summer months. I wanted a decree that would prevent him from being on the property except at my invitation so that I could rent the cottage and, with the income, pay taxes and maintenance and, above all, so that I could live with the children in some kind of peace. And, if he were to die, as the doctors said, I wanted to be in the position of being his widow so that I would have a claim to the property, his only remaining asset.

Even though I was not a lawyer—in the coming months I was to rue that unfortunate fact—it all seemed a perfectly reasonable, right and simple proposition to me. The only stumbling block was getting the money to pay a lawyer, as I knew Sean would never hand the house over to me unless he was forced to do so legally.

In addition to its being his only remaining asset, the East Hampton house had become a kind of holy land to him, his own inviolate piece of earth, a place to make his last stand. If I had had the money to go any place else and if I could have been sure that he would keep the house for us and also that he would keep it from going totally to rack and ruin, I would willingly have hied myself and the children elsewhere; but such was not the case. Despite his affection for it, there was always the possibility of his selling the house in either a drunken or desperate situation and, alimony laws to the contrary, skipping off with the proceeds, so that I would end up with neither the house nor the money. If we were divorced, there was also the possibility that he might re-marry, giving his second wife the chance to lay claim to the property when he died or, conceivably, sued for divorce. And although he had left the house to me in his will, made when the children were small and life was serene, I had no way of knowing whether or not he had changed his mind and cut me out, as he had threatened to do, and I wanted to remain married to him (but legally separated from him) to be in a better position to contest his will had he changed it. Nor did I see how he could possibly pay the taxes unless he rented the small cottage (and who but another down-and-out drinker could stand the ambiance), so that the house could be lost, sold at a nominal price at a sheriff's sale.

Dollar signs were bouncing around the walls as I sat in my jeweler's office, occasionally intercepting someone looking to buy or sell precious gems, searching my mind for words to convey the urgency of spending to buy the beautiful-person image, mulling over my legal problems all the while. I recalled that Bert had stated a fee of fifteen hundred dollars for a separation suit, plus expenses; it suddenly occurred to me that, rather than spending money I didn't have for a lawyer, I'd be better off going to Legal Aid. I didn't know much about this organization, other than that it was for people who couldn't afford to pay lawyers and that it was partially staffed by young associates of the better Wall Street firms, not shysters but men with the best training, lawyers who would appreciate my position and be able to resolve my problems —for free.

I called a friend who had done a great deal of fund-raising volunteer work for Legal Aid (her husband was a patent lawyer) and told her of my brainstorm. She agreed that it was a terrific idea and said she would call the head man to pave the way. I then called him, anticipating tones of warm, fatherly concern.

Instead he was very brusque, as if irritated by my call. I briefly described my situation—lawyer-husband now in a mental institution, four children, no money—when he interrupted to ask if I was entitled to Legal Aid services.

"I would certainly think so," I said. "I haven't a dime of my own." In a voice that indicated he was occupied with more pressing matters, he told me he would contact one of the lawyers on his staff and, giving me her name, told me to call her that afternoon.

He must have told her that I was a friend of one of the volunteers and thus akin to the idle rich, because if he sounded preoccupied, she sounded hysterical. As I started to explain that I had no money, husband in a mental hospital, four children, she interrupted in a piercing, aggravated voice to say, "We've got many sorely troubled people here and there isn't time—" at which point I interrupted her to snarl that I was also a sorely troubled person, looking for a legal remedy and needing help.

"Well, sometimes there aren't any remedies," she screeched, "and if your husband is in a mental hospital he's a sick man."

"I know he's a sick man," I answered through clenched teeth, "but he's also an alcoholically sick man—do you have any clue as to what that means?—and when he gets out of the hospital he's going to move right back in with us unless I have some legal way to keep him out."

"Are there children?" she snapped.

"I just told you there were four, all minors," I snapped back.

"All right, come to see me tomorrow afternoon," she said grudgingly, "but don't expect to come down here and get in front of others. You'll have to wait your turn."

"I don't expect to get in front of others," I answered, wondering how the downtrodden ever got a nickel's worth of advice from this bitch. "I'm simply looking for help, and that's what I thought Legal Aid was for."

I took the subway downtown and found the building. It was a blistering, white-hot, ninety-four-degree day, the kind of New York day to put one in a near trance. After paying a dollar fee for a card entitling me to Legal Aid services—so it said—I settled down in the waiting room, prepared to wait until hell froze over for my turn. I counted twenty-one people ahead of me. Seven were black women, two were white girls who looked to be under eighteen, another was a young white woman with her mother and fretful baby, whom they kept passing back and forth between them, and the rest were Puerto Rican men and women. They all looked poor, like people who had never known what it was to live in a beautiful place by the sea, people who were conditioned to wait forever for anything or nothing to happen. Underneath my ninety-dollar linen dress (being a size 10, I could buy expensive clothes on sale, and this dress, bought for my party-clinic work, had been in the cleaners when Sean ripped up my clothes) I was wearing my only remaining pair of pants and bra, and I may well have been as broke as anyone in the room. But I knew I was in no sense as poor; there had been too many good things in my life: parents who, despite their marital problems, had always stood behind me, an education, wonderful friends, and, most of all, the love of a warm and wonderful man. To pass the time I pulled my notebook out and went to work on my position paper.

An hour later a well-dressed woman of about my age came into the room and, glaring in my direction, asked my name and then beckoned me to follow. She listened impassively as I again recited my problems and my need for a legal separation.

"A separation? Why don't you want a divorce?" she asked bluntly.

I explained that I was trying to keep control of my husband's property.

"You have property?" she snapped. "Then we can't help you. If you have property, you have to pay for a lawyer."

"But I don't have property. It's in his name, not mine," I said.

"If your husband has property, then Legal Aid can't get involved. You'll just have to get the money from somewhere to pay a lawyer. Maybe you should have a public sale of the house. If your husband can't pay the taxes and you don't, the town will eventually put the house up for public sale and you can make the lawyer's fee contingent on the money received from the sale," she said affirmatively.

"That would take a year, and the house would be sold for less than its value and the money would go to my husband, and to get at it would mean more legal fees, less money for the children's support," I argued.

She shrugged. "You have to be realistic. The house is his only asset. See that it's sold, and your lawyer will go after the money if it means his fee."

I thanked her and deposited my Legal Aid card in the wastebasket as I left. Riding uptown on the subway, I wondered how I had reached the age of forty-two still being so ignorant about so many matters, especially those pertaining to law and medicine. I never seemed to ask the right questions, and I always ended up getting the wrong answers.

Back I went to my original lawyer. I had not seen Bert in over a year and a half, and we greeted each other like old but not particularly long-lost friends.

"Well, my dear," he said as we settled down in his office, "what can we do for you?"

I gave him a brief rundown on what had happened since I returned from Florida and said that I wanted to reopen separation proceedings and with all due haste to prevent Sean from moving back in on us when he was released from the hospital. Bert leaned back in his chair, a slight smile on his face. "This is the third time —three strikes and he's out, is that it?" It was another one of his irritating little jokes. I reminded him that I had never received a single scrap of paper establishing my legal independence, either the first or the second time. "If I had, I wouldn't be sitting here now," I lied.

He countered, in a tone of genuine concern, that it was a damn shame nothing could be done to help the poor guy. "Isn't there anything anyone can do . . . his brothers?"

"Apparently not," I answered without a trace of a tremor.

He had learned his lesson from the meaningless Bellevue service and said that of course it would be difficult to serve separation papers while Sean was in the state hospital but that we'd get an Order of Protection to keep him from coming to the house when he was released. "That will be easy. He's recently shown violence and the police know about it should we need witnesses." No mention was made of a fee.

Sean had been in the hospital for over a month when Bert finally called to say that a hearing was scheduled in the Family Court of Suffolk County, midway between East Hampton and New York.

"I don't need to go with you, just tell what you told me, the police coming, the children being there, all that, and you'll get your Order of Protection. And one other thing," he added. "Don't arrive looking like you just left Saks Fifth Avenue. Wear something that looks poor but honest."

Another absurdity of the law: dressing up in costume, as if

179

the merits of my case depended on a masquerade. However, anxious to avoid the Legal Aid treatment, I settled on an old brown silk and, without make-up or accessories, felt I looked appropriately drab and miserable.

When he was an Assistant U. S. Attorney, Sean had spent a certain amount of time in the Family Court in Manhattan and said it was badly organized, overcrowded, drab, dirty, full of poor confused people and too many bad lawyers. I expected the worst at the Family Court I was going to, but to my surprise it was clean and airy and also practically deserted. A young woman at a reception desk politely asked me to be seated, and in a matter of minutes a smiling man, middle-aged, who identified himself as the Court Clerk, came out and asked me if I would please step into his office. He was the soul of sympathy as he listened to my sad tale, and when I had finished he told me to wait outside and not to worry. Fifteen minutes later he called me in to sign the statement he had prepared, and I asked him, plaintively, if he thought I'd get my order.

"We aren't supposed to comment, but I'm almost sure there won't be any problems in your case," he answered with a fatherly smile. I thanked him for all he had done, smiled bravely, and tottered off to my car. Driving home, I felt tough and strong; something had finally happened, although I still wasn't quite sure what.

But it was not an easily sustained mood. Playing the hard-nosed role is only a bit better than sitting and stewing, hoping and praying. I had made up my mind to turn my back on my alcoholic, but it was a hard decision to live with, and though I had gotten Sean out of my life, I couldn't get him out of my mind.

When he had first been committed I had called the hospital several times to be told his condition was satisfactory. Toward the end of the second week I spoke to a doctor who said that my husband had appeared to be much better until he was found wandering on another floor of the hospital, totally disoriented and very frightened. Then, shortly thereafter, a notice came saying he had been transferred out of the hospital and into another building, so I assumed he was better, at least physically, though I feared to think what it would do to him to be incarcerated again with "the real nuts."

Sean called once to tell me to bring his glasses, clothes and money, all said in a peremptory but shaky voice. Hearing him made me want to cry, but I made myself sound firm and detached, saying I'd leave everything he wanted at the admissions building but that I could not and would not see him. He asked how I could be such a cold bitch after all we had meant to each other. I said I was sorry and hung up, feeling very like a cold bitch, cold and old and dried up with grieving; but there was no longer any middle ground left in which to help him and help the children and myself at the same time, and I knew that a single visit would wipe out my resolution to get free of him. I was especially depressed on his birthday when he turned forty-four.

Trying to think through the coming year, I decided there was no alternative but to continue to live in the country, even though I hadn't a clue as to how I could work there and earn enough to support the children. East Hampton being primarily a summer resort, wintertime jobs were hard to come by. But the negatives in New York were financially insurmountable. I knew I could find a job there but not one with a salary commensurate with the expenses of living there. Rents had escalated, as had school tuitions, and I was afraid to live in a cheap neighborhood, if such existed, and to put the children in public schools. I had called the headmaster of their former school to be told that in terms of scholarship funds my children were, unfortunately, the wrong color, as the school was now reaching out to ghetto students. I wondered whether it would have helped if their father had been a black alcoholic; probably not, a drunk being anathema whatever his color. With his usual verbosity and perhaps a ploy to drive me off for all time, the headmaster had asked me in shocked tones if I knew that my husband had come to the school and made a terrible scene in his office and the school lobby when I had taken the children away to Florida, and I knew that in no circumstances did he want my alcoholic's children back in his school again.

Wintertime rents in East Hampton were reasonable, and, if not as stimulating as independent city schools, those in East Hampton were at least peaceful and I wouldn't have to worry about muggings or other such hazards. As for earning our keep, I'd just have to trust to luck. I signed a lease for a three-bedroom house, a bit tacky but near the schools, and only one hundred fifty a month, available September 15. This made it essential to initiate my legal separation before Sean was released at the end of September so that he couldn't move in on us. Without heat in our own house, he'd then be forced by the cold to leave East Hampton and return to his apartment in the city, thus protecting the children from another year of living in a small town where their father was becoming very visibly a town drunk. (I had paid three hundred and sixty dollars in back rent so that he would have a place to go when he got out.) However, it was now August, and still nothing had happened legally. I called Bert to stress the urgency of my action.

Alas, my lawyer, like the headmaster, wanted no part of our messy situation.

"Look," he counseled over the phone, "if you're going to be living in another county, you'd be much better off if you sue out there. The calendars here are jammed. Get a local lawyer. He'll know the judges and you'll get much faster action." Three strikes and I, not my husband, was out. That was the last time I ever talked to Bert.

I was referred to a lawyer in a town thirty miles away, said to be an expert in marital matters. Being by now fairly disenchanted with the legal profession and hoping to avoid confusion and wasted time, I wrote a concise summary of my situation, spelling out precisely why I wanted a separation and not a divorce, what I wanted to achieve, and stressing the urgency of my situation. I pointed out that delays with my previous lawyer had stemmed from the difficulty of serving the necessary papers on my husband, noting that service on him at Bellevue had been dismissed *vis-à-vis* serving him now when he was a patient in the state hospital.

Several days later he called. "Lady," he chortled over the phone, "you've got problems." We made a date for two days hence.

As I drove the thirty miles to his office I remembered my first nervous, sad attempt three years before to find a legal solution to my husband's alcoholism, the near-tearful interview in the elegant office of Lawyer Number One, the taxi ride to the wrong side of the legal tracks where I was palmed off on Lawyer Number Two, a forlorn, ambivalent, lost soul, trusting that I would find a mentor with the wisdom, experience, and training to help me through my difficulties. Now I was approaching my new savior, Lawyer Number Three, in a mood akin to contempt.

He was a partner in a firm with dignified offices, a man in his late thirties, with a quick, nervous way of speaking. He had my letter before him.

"Why do you want a separation? With the new laws, it's much easier to get a divorce," said the man whom I shall call Mr. Eaton.

"Did you bother to read the letter through?" I asked patiently.

He glanced down at it quickly and then said, "Why don't you want him to sell the house? Then he could pay alimony and child support. This way, according to what you say, he hasn't any money and isn't about to earn some."

I suggested he read the letter again. After doing so he said that he would take the case for a fee of seven hundred and fifty dollars, "Payable in three easy installments," and that as soon as he received a check for two hundred and fifty dollars proceedings would begin. I asked when I could expect a decree.

"It shouldn't take more than three months," he answered airily, "by mid-November at the latest."

"But what good does that do?" I demanded. "My husband will get out of the hospital in September, move in on me, and I'll be right back where I started."

"Then we'll immediately file for a custody order. We'll show the court he's a drunken bum, that he shouldn't be around the kids. It really is very bad, and the first thing you know one of the boys is going to be in trouble with the law. It happens over and over—parent becomes a drunken bum, kid becomes a delinquent."

"My husband is not a drunken bum, he's an alcoholic," I countered defensively, "and my children have done extremely well in the circumstances." I had to defend them against this male Cassandra, even though I had heard rumors that young Sean and Curtis were smoking marijuana. It was the peak of the drug culture, and I was terrified for them, knowing how vulnerable they were. They denied it and, being saturated with the problems of alcoholism, I chose to believe them.

I told Mr. Eaton I had already been through the Order of Protection procedure but had never received a legal document to that effect and asked him to contact my previous lawyer. I also asked him to make sure of the meaning of the document, as I wasn't looking for custody of the children but a means of keeping my husband away from them and from me.

"Don't worry," he answered affirmatively, "you've got a good case and we'll get you the right order. That will be an additional two hundred and fifty, so make the first check for five hundred, plus twenty-five for service, five twenty-five in all."

"If everyone knows it's harmful to have an alcoholic father around his children and if I've got such a good case, why is it so expensive?" I asked coldly. I recalled reading somewhere that in Japan one could get a divorce for a dollar.

"Best investment you ever made." He laughed. I didn't like his smart-alecky wit, but he seemed aggressive and confident and I left convinced that my problems would soon be solved.

In actual fact, however, nine months were to elapse before my "good case" was resolved.

I never knew what became of my original visit to the Family Court (nor did I ever receive a bill from Bert), and to a large extent I never knew quite what was happening, being constantly buffeted by documents from the Family Court, the state hospital, my lawyer, all written in legalese and none making much sense to me, a non-lawyer.

My first court document, entitled "Order to Show Cause," dated August 22, stated that services on the respondent had been made informing him that on September 22 in the County Supreme Court said respondent was to "show cause" why an order should not be made "awarding custody of the infants to the petitioner herein" and directing the respondent to "be enjoined from removing said infants from the control, care and custody of your petitioner . . . and for such other and further relief as to the Court may seem just and proper, and that in the interim and pending the further order of this court, that said respondent be and he hereby is enjoined from interfering with the custody and control of the petitioner over said infants."

My Order to Show Cause was granted in answer to my petition "For the Determination of the Custody" of the children, which, after noting the history of my husband's alcoholism, stated that "the best interests of said infant children would be protected by said infant children's remaining in the sole care, control and custody of your petitioner." Neither document said that my husband was not to come into our home, only that he be "enjoined from interfering."

Attached to the Order to Show Cause was a photostat of an "Affidavit of Personal Service," signed by a doctor associated with the state hospital and sworn before a notary public, stating service on both my husband and the director of the hospital. (Why, I wondered, hadn't Bert used this method of service on my husband when he was in Bellevue?) This meant that Sean had seen and presumably read the documents.

Other than the one phone call early in the summer I had had no communication from him except a few lines written on a scrap of paper—literally a scrap, not a sheet—saying he loved me, was terribly bored, missed the children, and longed for the taste of red, ripe August tomatoes and a swim in the cold sea. I wouldn't let myself cry.

In September I received a second call. Sean sounded remote but very calm as he said he would be getting out in ten days and would let me know when to come and get him. "I can't come and get you, Sean," I said carefully and quietly. "Our marriage is over." I told him I'd send him money to get to New York and see that all of his clothes and things were delivered to his apartment but that I could not and would not come to get him, nor was he to come to East Hampton, as his visit would serve no purpose other than to upset me and the children.

"I'm coming home," he answered, "and there's nothing you can do about it."

"Oh, yes there is," I answered, my voice rising. "I have a custody order, and if you come here I'll call the police and they'll make you leave."

"That's a phony, meaningless document. It's my house, remember, not yours, and I'll come when I choose, and there's nothing you can do about it, legally or illegally." After adding something to the effect that he didn't know how I could constantly come up with such knuckleheads for lawyers, he hung up.

I called my brother-in-law in Boston to ask if he could possibly meet Sean when he was released and take him to the city. He said he was too involved in a trial but would try to get to see him as soon as possible. Then I called Mr. Eaton to report my husband's opinion of my custody order. He assured me that all I need do was to call the police, show them the order, and my husband would have to leave.

However much I dreaded an encounter, I felt it would be wrong to sic the police on Sean the minute he stepped out of the hospital, so instead of taking my prized document to the station I braced myself for his arrival, knowing that in a matter of days we would be moving into the house I had rented for the winter and thus be safe on our own territory. If nothing else, I had learned not to panic, and I told the children that Daddy might be coming for a short visit, a few days in which he could collect his things before returning to his New York apartment. They knew of my separation plans, and I feared that an unexpected, unannounced visit from their father would add to their confusion and turmoil.

He arrived around nine one evening, a shabby figure dressed in odds and ends issued by the hospital. The big Newfoundland, his tail wagging joyfully, jumped up, putting his front paws on my husband's shoulders.

"Daddy!" the children gasped. "How did you get here?"

"Hi, boys," he said, laughing softly, hugging the dog as he pushed him down. "I walked . . . and I'm tired." The children watched in awkward silence.

He sank down on the Eames chair (we had bought it in Washington one lovely spring afternoon while meandering around Georgetown) and for the first time looked directly at me as I sat, immobilized, on the couch. With a half-defiant smile he said quietly, "Have you anything to drink?"

I shook my head, remembering how I had once admired his bravura.

"Would you like some dinner?" I asked as calmly as possible.

It was a difficult but not impossible two days. Other than at mealtimes, and these were strained, I stayed out of his way, ferrying things over to the rented house and doing errands, any-thing to keep my mind off loving him. He didn't appear to be drinking and certainly looked much better, clear-eyed and trim. But there was a furtive, withdrawn quality about him that was disturbing. Having gone into the state hospital a madman, he had come out, ninety days later, acting like a hunted man, almost a criminal.

On the Sunday we were to move he left the house at noon and hadn't returned by the time we made the final trip to our winter rental. It was a small house and rather shabby, but it seemed miraculously warm and cozy by comparison with our unheated one. The boys kept saying, "This is great, Mom" as they settled in for a peaceful evening of watching TV. All was serene until eight, when my husband called in a rage to say that if we didn't return the television immediately he'd break every window in the house. I knew he would and I'd have to pay for the repairs, so despite their protests I drove it and the older boys over to the house and they put the set inside the front door.

I heard no more, and a week later I went back to the house certain that his silence meant that he had left and I could retrieve the television. It was upstairs in our bedroom, the bed unmade and dirty, two empty bottles on the floor beside it, along with a pan with burned beans stuck to it. His clothes were gone.

On the bedside table was a memorandum from the state hospital addressed to To Whom It May Concern. It gave my husband's name and hospital number and said, "This verifies that Patient is discharged today from this Hospital.

"Given property, no money, no medication, no after-care clinic." It was signed by a doctor and dated.

The forgotten man had been dismissed, free to go his dismal, downward way.

～ 14 ～

Fighting for a New Life
Winter 1968–1969

I had run out of my summer free-lance jobs and wanted to get the boys established in school before pursuing others. Free-lancing was a chancy way to survive, and as fall began I weighed alternatives. Financially I was in a complete bind. I could neither sell nor mortgage the house because it wasn't in my name. To my knowledge there were no jobs in East Hampton other than as cleaning woman or expert typist, and in neither area did I qualify. A full-time job in New York meant a full-time housekeeper in the country, and even if I could have found one the expense, combined with my living expenses in town, would cancel out my salary. And most of all I didn't want to leave the boys five days a week.

Magically, my fairy godmother, Marjorie, reappeared. During the summer I had contacted my former boss at the public-relations firm, and in early October she called to ask if I could "help out" by working three days a week for the usual fifty a day.

This meant no taxes, and it also meant I had to spend only two nights a week in town. The six-thirty morning train got me in by ten on Tuesdays, and the Thursday-night train brought me back to East Hampton by ten. I hired a high-school girl to come after school and spend the night, so with all expenses combined I was still able to clear around seventy-five a week, enough to cover weekly expenses but not enough to pay rent, fuel, utilities, insurance premiums, and certainly not the mortgage. I wrote my father (he had already given me five hundred to pay the lawyer) and my sister's husband and Sean's brother Dan, and once again they responded generously, with Dan even volunteering to pay the mortgage. (I don't know what would have happened if I hadn't had relatives who cared. I wasn't too proud to ask for welfare, but in the circumstances I doubt that we could have qualified.)

I shall always be grateful to those who gave me bed and board the nights I was in town. I became an apartment bum, with my own set of rules and regulations for being one in the most inconspicuous and least troublesome way I knew. Among my rules: Never spend two nights in the same apartment more than once a month; arrange to be elsewhere on one of the two nights, unless the host family was itself going to be out; never leave clothes behind (by the end of the second month I found it simpler to leave a change of clothes in my office and carry only a tote bag with toothbrush, robe, change of underwear to that week's apartment); never get up when the host family was breakfasting and getting off to work and school; always carry my own alarm clock; never, no matter how sincere the offer, accept an invitation to sleep on the living-room couch (I did spend one miserable night in a junior bed, a good five inches shorter than I was); and whenever the opportunity arose, cancel all else to stay in an empty apartment.

I regularly took sleeping pills to be able to sleep in my series of strange beds, and at first I found it disorienting to waken in the morning and not immediately remember where I was. But after a while I didn't care; it was always a nice place. Though I constantly worried about the children's well-being, in some ways bumming was fun, providing an elegant change of scene and a refreshing look into more ordered lives (and sometimes a look into lives that were less ordered than they appeared to be at a safer distance). It was also a tiring life, being a floating house guest combined with getting up before dawn to catch a train for three hard days' work, coming home late two nights later, and spending the next four days trying to shore up the boys, emotionally and hygienically—the high-school girl was a hopeless housekeeper. Yet it was a more ordered and peaceful life. I felt I had done the right thing in pushing my alcoholic out and looked to the day when our separation would be legally established. The day, however, was rapidly receding into the distance.

I had understood my lawyer to say that my husband would be served with separation papers *as he left the hospital* (perhaps the knock-out punch, but having made up my mind to be tough, I agreed). Several weeks after the date of the supposed service, I received a letter from Eaton stating that the process server had been unable to locate my husband, so unless I had a better suggestion, service of the separation papers would have to wait until Sean appeared in court for the custody-order hearing. (At this point my only legal document was a temporary custody order, and in my confusion—coupled with the tiring way of my life— it didn't occur to me to ask why Sean hadn't been served with separation papers when he had been served with the custody order.) The custody-order hearing, however, had been put off until the end of November. As usual, Sean had pulled his legal mind together and asked for a postponement until that date. So, having originally contacted Eaton in mid-August, all I had to show for my five hundred and twenty-five dollars by the end of October was the temporary custody order.

Returning from the city one cold Thursday night at ten, I opened the front door to find my alcoholic stretched out on the

191

living-room couch, his bottle beside him and the boys staring solemnly at the TV—a grim tableau from the preceding year. I could see that the boys were upset. They said Daddy had dismissed the baby-sitter, burned the dinner he had tried to cook for them, and they were now starving. My husband opened his eyes, smiled his drunken smile, and said, "Welcome home." I was too tired and too unnerved and didn't want to upset the children further, so instead of immediately calling the police I decided to hold my fire until the following day when they would be off in school.

The next morning I marched to the police station with my temporary custody order. The lieutenant on duty looked at the document and said he didn't see where it said my husband couldn't come into the house, only that I had custody of the children, and, as I was still his legal wife, he couldn't remove my husband from the premises. I pointed out the "enjoined from interfering" phrase, and he shrugged his shoulders. A detective was then called in to give a careful reading to my document and, having done so, he announced that the document was a custody order and that meant I had custody of the children.

I called Eaton. He was unavailable, in court for the day. I asked the policeman to call a local judge. The judge said he'd have to read the order, and one of the policemen drove me to his office. Local judges did not have to be lawyers in East Hampton, and this one was not. He pondered my document and, after reading it through several times, looked up and said, "This is a custody order. It says you have custody of the children. But it doesn't say your husband can't come into the house."

"It says he is 'enjoined from interfering' . . . right there," I answered, trying hard to contain myself, "and he is definitely interfering. It's my house, not his. The lease is in my name only."

The judge read my paper again and then said he could do nothing until he talked to my lawyer. I went home and told Sean he'd have to leave. He laughed. I didn't mention my custody order; I felt like too much of a fool.

By the time I got through to my lawyer the following morning (this meant leaving the house to make a secret call) I was livid and demanded to know why he had charged me two hundred and fifty dollars for a useless piece of paper.

"The paper's not the problem. The problem is that you're dealing with a bunch of idiots," he answered, then assured me he would call the judge and straighten matters out. I told him to send the process server over immediately with the separation papers. Eaton said that was a great idea but, being Saturday, he couldn't get a process server and instead he would mail the papers and for five dollars I could get a cop to serve them on my husband the following Monday. But when I returned to my house Sean was gone.

He was back again, however, the next Thursday night, and without taking off my coat I went straight upstairs and called the police. The message had gotten through as to the meaning of my custody order, and the man on duty said he would dispatch two men right away. I called to the children to come upstairs and told them to wait there until the episode was over, and then I went back down, my heart pounding. I hated doing what I was doing. When the officers came to the door I said I didn't want my husband arrested, only made to leave my house. Our voices awakened Sean. He said he was not leaving, that I was still his legal wife, although he feared I was now a little crazy.

"I'm afraid you'll have to come with us, sir," one of the officers said. "Don't make it difficult."

The strait-jacket scene flashed through my mind, and I ran upstairs, where the children were waiting, wide-eyed, and closed the bedroom door.

"Is Daddy being arrested?" Seamus asked, smiling the way children sometimes do when they are confused and frightened. I shook my head, no.

The flashing police lights shot through the window, then they disappeared and Sean was gone. I had forgotten to have him served with the separation papers. The next morning I took them to the police station, knowing he would be back; and late in the afternoon, when I went into the kitchen to start dinner, there he was, standing by the open refrigerator door, foraging.

"Don't you have anything to eat in this goddamned house?" he said. I didn't answer. "And don't try that police routine again or you'll be dead," he announced matter-of-factly, drunk but in a sober, authoritative way. His high-handedness made my gorge rise, but I kept silent, waiting for my chance to act.

We were strangers in the neighborhood, so I waited until dark when the neighbors and the children playing in the school yard across the street wouldn't have such a clear view and then called the police again. When they arrived one of them touched my husband with the separation papers and said that he was served. I felt a small sense of triumph. I had succeeded where my lawyers had failed; I had finally outsmarted my alcoholic. But I told the police again that I didn't want him arrested, only removed.

Saturday morning as I was driving off to market I saw him coming up the street toward the house. No longer caring what the neighbors thought, I drove directly to the police station and asked that he be removed again, and when I returned from the shopping the children told me the police had come and taken Daddy away. (These were our beautiful babies, each of whom was to have a golden childhood, and this was what I was doing to them.) The whole Kafkaesque episode left me hollow, and while routinely putting the groceries away I said as evenly as I could that Daddy was too sick to know what he was doing and I was trying to do what I thought best. And then I suggested that we drive to Montauk and picnic by the lighthouse. Maybe nature would soothe the wounds.

Monday morning, after the children were in school, the door burst open and my alcoholic was inside. He yanked the phone from the jack and threw it out the door and, eyes blazing, said he'd kill me if I tried to leave. Still hollow, drained and bloodless, I continued the housework as he followed me from room to room, telling me he loved me, that I was mad to think I could ever leave him, and intermittently asking for a drink. I had shown him my empty Scotch bottle in the trash, and at noon he told me to drive him to the liquor store, escorting me to the car with a kitchen knife. But when we arrived there was no way he could make me come with him and no way to get the liquor without leaving me, and as soon as he went inside I dashed from the car and ran for the police station. The officer on duty said he would no longer baby-sit my husband, and he refused to send a policeman after him unless I signed a complaint for his arrest. Then he could be shipped off to the county jail.

"He doesn't belong in jail—he belongs in a hospital," I said.

"We don't have anything to do with that. Talk to the judge. You have to go there to sign the complaint," he answered.

It was the same judge I had seen about my custody order, and when I asked him why my husband couldn't be sent back to the hospital he was his usual taciturn self. He said nothing, his way of dealing with problems he didn't understand. "Does he have to go to jail?" I repeated. "Why?"

"Do you want him out of your house?" he answered, indicating where I was to sign.

"How long?" I asked.

"We'll give him fifteen days. But it can be suspended."

I signed, a robot, and the officer took me home, first searching the house, then leaving to track down Sean. I sat on the couch, depleted, paralyzed by the hideous reality. If only the man I loved had had any disease other than alcoholism, any sickness that could be treated other than as a crime!

The police called at four that afternoon to say they were still unable to locate my husband. Twenty minutes later, as I was driving Seamus to the dentist, I saw Sean walking up the street toward our house. He had changed into his navy-blue blazer and gray flannels, and other than the thin trickle of blood coming from his nose he looked presentable.

"There's Daddy!" Seamus exclaimed. I drove faster and

dropped him at the dentist's and then went to the drugstore to call the police. There was nothing I could do about the other three boys at home, but I couldn't bear to have Seamus—our lovely, loving son—witness his father's arrest, and after his appointment I drove him to the beach. It was growing dark and there was a strong wind, and I watched as he jumped about, laughing as he dodged the waves of the roiling sea, almost as if he were putting on a little show to cheer me up. When we returned home Curtis said quietly, "Daddy came back, Mom, and the police came with handcuffs."

I called Eaton early in December. He assured me that despite the delays in service and the interruptions to be caused by the coming holidays, I could expect a decree in January. That was good news, one of the few happy thoughts for the coming Christmas season. It takes a holiday to point up the desperate messes of our lives, and with no money to spend on gifts and with the children left on their own in the country, out of school and with nothing to do while I did my work in the city, it was hard to figure out how this Christmas could be less than dismal. The boys were lonely and restless in the country (our way of life made it difficult for them to be outgoing and friendly with the other kids in school, and they kept to themselves) and wanted to come into the city to see old friends, but it was a problem to find places for all of them to stay when everyone was coming home from school to fill up extra bedrooms; and it was also difficult to find a bed for myself. Jack, an old friend of Sean's, solved that problem by saying I could use his company's apartment, vacant for the holidays, and the gift problem was considerably improved when my PR firm lost a major manufacturer of games as a client. Marjorie told me to help myself to the office supply, all brand new, and as they were meant to be used for promotion, all were in super-deluxe packaging. There was another joyful windfall when I opened a Christmas card from Laura Lee, a former Bennington classmate and close friend but one I hadn't seen in several years. Tucked inside was a hundred-dollar bill.

In the happier, bygone days I had always sent gifts to the children of my husband's brothers and sister. They had done the same, and part of the excitement of Christmas was watching these mysterious packages mount under the tree. This year I couldn't afford to buy the requisite eleven gifts and instead sent a picture of Sean's four sons. It was a good photograph, an unposed close-up taken on the wintery, bleak beach, and it caught in the four pairs of eyes a cast of the strain and confusion they were going through. I hoped it would remind my in-laws that whatever they thought of me or their brother, it was our children who were the innocent victims. Not only did the mysterious, exciting packages continue to arrive that year, but the gifts were the most carefully selected of any that had ever been sent. There were other presents from my sister and from friends who didn't want the boys to feel bereft; and they didn't. They had put on a brave front, saying presents didn't matter—they knew how broke we were—but when they began to arrive they were elated by the vast array, and Christmas turned out to be better than they had anticipated.

When the boys came into the city, Nicholas, who had worried what Daddy would do about Christmas when we ran off to Florida, asked me for ten dollars to buy Daddy a gift. He said he wanted to get his father a pair of gloves "to keep him warm" and, having made the purchase, said we should all go to see him. I knew Sean was in his apartment, and though I was reluctant to see him, I thought it would be good psychologically for the children to have some kind of relationship, provided their father was relatively pulled together. I called him and asked if we could come by the following morning (assuming this might be his most sober time of day); he sounded surprised to hear from me but delighted with the idea.

I went along only to assure myself that it was safe to leave the younger boys with him, and he seemed fine when he met us at the door, clean-shaven and neatly dressed. There were no recriminations about jail, no mention of it, and we both behaved like a perfectly normal separated couple doing their best to make it a happier holiday for the children. I kept my coat on to maintain my identity as a visitor, and after ten minutes I said I had to be on my way to work, and he walked out to the elevator with me. He put his arm around me and said he hoped it would be a better new year for both of us, and I asked if he needed money to take the boys to lunch and gave him six dollars, all I could spare.

That evening Seamus told me that they had gone to the zoo in Central Park and afterward had met a lady friend of Daddy's, whom he described as being much taller and much younger than Daddy and also rich.

"How did you know she was rich?" I asked.

"Because she had a fur coat and a French poodle," he explained matter-of-factly.

I was glad Sean had a girl friend; maybe she could help or, if nothing else, save him from loneliness. My own was assuaged by the children and also by staying with friends in the city and seeing summer people who continued to come for winter weekends in the country.

January was a busy month. I took young Sean, who was restless in the public high school, on two short tours of New England prep schools, hoping he could get a scholarship for the following year. In addition to my three-day-a-week job I was still doing my teen-party clinics for Manny, who sent me off to Pittsburgh. (While I was there the public-relations man assigned to cart me about to radio and TV stations told me with great enthusiasm that he was doing publicity for a new book. Its title was *Feel Fit on a Fifth a Day: The Defensive Drinker's Diet.* I never commented on the subject matter, just thanked him when he gave me a copy inscribed "Best Wishes and Bottoms UP.") So with all the activity, including the regular concerns of running a house, I neglected to hound my lawyer, and it wasn't until the end of the month that I realized that the promised separation hearing had never materialized.

I wrote him a testy letter (he was always out when I called) and received a reply that the hearing was now scheduled for March. The letter further noted that as I had paid five hundred and twenty-five dollars "on account of our fees and disbursements," including a fee for the custody order "in the amount of $350," would I now kindly forward a check in the amount of two hundred dollars.

Recalling that he had originally said the custody order would be two hundred and fifty dollars, not three hundred and fifty dollars, I decided I was dealing not merely with a nincompoop but, worse, a crook. Why, I wondered, hadn't I had the sense to ask for a written financial agreement?

I wrote back, suggesting he review his bookkeeping and reminding him that over five months had elapsed since my original visit, at which time he had told me that my "good case" would be resolved in three months and that therefore I saw no reason whatsoever to pay him another cent, as nothing had been accomplished. And then, hedging but sniping at the same time, I asked if he intended to prolong the delays unless I sent the money.

I immediately received an apology for the oversight in bookkeeping and his assurance that my case was being given every consideration, with or without further payment; the delay was due entirely to the crowded court calendars, and would I be kind enough to sign the enclosed conciliation papers, a mere formality that came into being with the revised state laws on divorce and separation agreements. The letter noted that it would take only a few weeks to get the conciliation papers properly filed.

Why, I wondered, if they were a mere formality, had he not sent the conciliation papers a long time ago? I signed them and to be on the safe side enclosed a check for two hundred and then went on about my other affairs.

Although the wheels of the law seemed destined to grind down to a halt, life improved considerably when, on March 1, I started work in East Hampton at the local cultural center. The

199

salary for five days was less than I made working three in New York, but the luxury of staying home more than equalized the difference, both financially and emotionally. I had just about had it as an apartment bum (as I'm sure my friends also had), and I knew the arrangement was not good for the children, especially the youngest. Seamus still had serious reading problems and was doing poorly in school and in the afternoons often came home to an empty house. The Newfoundland dog, his loyal companion, had been run over by a truck (more devastating sadness), and the baby-sitter had become increasingly less reliable, sometimes not showing up at all. The boys all coped marvelously, getting themselves up and off to school in the morning and cooking dinner as directed in the notes I left for the sitter, but there were obviously too many loose ends in their lives, and the makeshift arrangements were wearing them down.

Another boost came when young Sean received a full scholarship to prep school for the following fall. From the five first-rate schools we had visited, he received three offers of aid, including one for the full $4,000 tuition. It was good for his ego and the family morale in general.

March was given over to settling into my new job and having Seamus's tonsils removed, and at the end of the month I realized again that nothing had transpired legally. I called Eaton's office to learn from his secretary that he was taking a much-needed two-week vacation. In April I went first to Florida and then back to Pittsburgh on my party-clinic job (I had made this a condition of my new job; I was now earning a hundred dollars a day pushing snacks and had told my employer it was necessary compensation for the meager salary offered), and it was suddenly the first of May. Abandoning all attempts to be civil, I called my lawyer and asked him what in the hell was the matter with him. He said the court calendars were very crowded.

"I don't think that's the reason at all," I snapped. "I think it's because you're very remiss as a lawyer and the delay was caused because you forgot to send me the conciliation papers a long time ago. Isn't that the real reason?"

Instead of answering my question he said, "Well, if you're that dissatisfied, you'd better get yourself another lawyer."

"I'll be goddamned if I will at this stage of the game," I snarled. "I've already paid you seven hundred and twenty-five dollars, and I've put up with your ineptness for eight solid months, and if something doesn't happen soon, I'm going straight to the newspapers with this story."

He mumbled that he'd see about getting the hearing moved up.

I then wrote him a reminder that the purpose of my suit was to get possession of my husband's house and that I would be moving back into it on May 15, when the lease on my rented one was up, and thus time was of the essence, as without legal means of keeping him off the property it followed as the night the day that my husband would reappear on the scene.

We moved in, and sure enough, on the first night of the Memorial Day weekend, after we had all gone to bed, I awakened to hear a banging at the door. The big bad wolf was back, pounding and shouting that if I didn't let him into his house he'd break down the door. I lay in bed, knowing it was futile to call the police because it was still his house and I had no legal means of keeping him out, knowing that he would indeed break down the door, knowing that once again there was nothing I could do, and, knowing this, I didn't move. Maybe it was all just a bad dream. Then Curtis, poor Curtis, who could never not hear the bad sounds of the night, was standing in my room, asking if he should go down and tell Daddy to leave.

"Go back to bed, honey," I answered. "It will be all right."

(A few weeks after his father died Curtis said to me, "I heard sounds last night, and when I first woke up I thought it was Daddy again, but then I realized I didn't have to worry anymore.")

"Don't make so much noise. You'll wake the children," I

said, opening the door. My once shining prince, now turned disreputable drunken reprobate, kicked it closed and told me he would do as he pleased in his own house and I could get the hell out. One fights fire with fire and madness with madness, so I shrugged and, seeing his bottle, went to the pantry for glasses. Alone in the middle of the night, without the children, the rest of the world sealed off in darkness, we settled down to drink and talk, easily, companionably, picking over the remnants of twenty years, an old-shoe bond no matter how shattered, as long as it could be lived in the secrecy of the night.

I told him about my job, and he told me that during the winter he had gone to his former law office's annual party, drunk and dressed in his ski clothes, and he had been thrown out. He told me about his girl friend, Marguerite, how he had gotten her on the pill and taught her about sex, but he wasn't going to see her anymore because he knew he was bad news and she was an innocent, a baby, and not tough like me.

"I made you tough," he said, laughing softly. "My beautiful girl has turned into the Wicked Witch of the East, out to get me. Remember the first letter you wrote me, saying you couldn't come to winter house parties? You gave three phony reasons why, and I decided you were just another New York bitch, and then you said something about the valentine I'd sent you, how it made you feel better all day, like a little girl, warm and sweet. That's what you were. Warm and sweet. And bonnie and bright. And trusting and true. I changed all that, turned you into a clutch fighter, Class A. Christ, you should have been in the infantry. But we had a lot of fun, didn't we?" He sighed deeply and shook his head. "Well, that doesn't matter now. Anyway, you'll survive. And all I care about is drinking and screwing. That's all that's left."

This was the college boy who wrote, "Remember, *you* make the breaks, nobody hands them to you," and the soldier who wrote, "I have confidence in myself and in 'the stars' and I know that whatever happens to me from here on will only be to my advantage." Around dawn he passed out, and at seven-thirty I quietly awakened the children and moved into a friend's house for the weekend. By Monday night he was gone.

I called Eaton and said he had to act, that my husband would be back and the next time he would stay. Eaton assured me the separation decree would be mine in a matter of days.

During the same week I received a short note from Sean. It made no reference to his visit the preceding weekend.

> To your disadvantage I am a survivor, easy to hurt, tough to kill. But my luck will soon run out as it does for all so just hang in there and all your problems will be over.
>
> In the meantime, I really need $100 pronto. I still have the problem of paying June rent. And at this point I do not have enough money for food, a needed haircut or, for that matter, a subway token. I need dental work and new glasses. Please do what you can for me.

I sent him fifty dollars, all I could spare. What he was living on was a mystery to me. His brother Dan, who sent me the monthly check, sometimes enclosed a note, but it rarely mentioned Sean; and other than the presents sent to the boys at Christmas, there had been no communication between myself and Sean's sister and other brother. I accepted their silence and apparent antipathy to me; it was a way of trying to forget the problem, perhaps their only defense against the pain and sorrow they felt for their brother's plight. Somewhere along the line I had come to believe that the brother who ignored my plea for help was paying Sean's rent, perhaps even a bit more, and that, with the small check he received each month as a partially disabled veteran (recompense for his World War II wounds), was his wherewithal for survival. Or, so I told myself, my defense. In matters alcoholic, it's best to look away.

And then I received a call from Marguerite.

"You don't know who this is," she began in a soft, tense voice, "but I'm a friend of your husband's and I'm terribly, terribly worried about him."

I asked if she was Marguerite and she said yes, how did I know, and then began to cry, saying she would never have dreamed of calling but someone had to help Sean and she didn't know to whom else she could turn. She sounded like such a nice girl, an innocent as Sean had said, and I told her I admired her for calling and for being Sean's friend and trying to help but that there was nothing I could do. I meant to sound resolute, as if I knew how to deal with the problem sensibly, but it had been so long since I had talked to anyone who cared as much as I and my defenses collapsed and I, too, started to cry. And then we both started to laugh because it was too much like a scene out of a bad movie. She said she was leaving for Europe in a few days because she couldn't stand to see Sean in such terrible shape, and I said I was getting a separation for the same reason, and we agreed that it was nice to have talked. (We never met, but after Sean died I found a letter she had written him saying no one would ever love him as much as she did; she was wrong about that, but I was glad he had had her love.)

Finally, in the middle of June, my lawyer called to say the date for the hearing was set and, par for the course, laughingly advised me not to wear a miniskirt but to look poor, humble, and dignified. I took the brown silk dress to the cleaners and set off for court looking appropriately drab and neat. As we drove sullenly along in his car, Eaton told me what questions he would ask me and what I was to answer, all of which were concerned with the ages, birthplace, etc., of the children, my husband's education, previous employment, drinking habits.

"But when are you going to ask him for possession of the house?" I demanded. "I've been telling you for the past nine months that's the main reason I want a separation."

"That's a tricky proposition," he said, explaining that since

our first object was to secure the separation decree, he would wait
to see what kind of a mood the judge was in. "It might jeopardize
the case to ask for the sole right. After all, it's wholly owned by
your husband."

"Why?" I argued. "My husband can't support me or the
children, and I can't possibly pay the big summer rents during the
season, and I can't quit my job to move someplace where the rents
are cheap but there's no work. If the judge can't understand that,
he's stupid and the law is absurd."

"You're wrong," he said, "because no matter how much of
a bastard a person is, one's private property is private property.
That's a fundamental law of this country and it's a good one. And
until he sells it or gives it to you, it's your husband's property,
period."

We arrived at the courthouse, and I was relieved when I
didn't see Sean; it made it easier to think I was doing a perfunctory act, a trip to the dentist.

A thin, pale nineteen-year-old, her voice barely audible, was
explaining that her husband of two years had deserted her a few
weeks after their marriage. "Like I never even slep' with him, or
nothin'," she said, and the judge granted her an annulment. Then
a thin, sallow man came on the stand to say he had been unfairly
deprived of his rights in prison and no longer had exercise privi-
leges. He had difficulty in expressing himself, and the judge was
very patient and tried to help him to say what he meant.

My lawyer whispered that the judge was in a good mood and
said he would ask for possession of the house.

When my turn came I swore to tell the whole truth and
nothing but: marriage, date and place; children, names and ages;
present address of myself and children; who supported the children.

My lawyer next asked where my husband had been educated,
his profession, when he had last worked and salary of his last job.
The judge, a man in his early fifties, took off his glasses and shook

his head in dismay. Eaton then asked how long my husband had been an alcoholic, when and where he had been committed, and the manner in which he attempted to break into my sister's house one year ago. The judge frowned and shook his head and then spoke. With wisdom dating back to the time of Solomon, he pronounced it a disgrace for a man with my husband's education and with a family to support to behave as he had. He said it was irresponsible.

My lawyer then asked if I could have possession of my husband's house, as I had no other place to live and care for the children. The judge said he would certainly take that possibility under consideration, and I knew we had won.

I had tried for three years to find a legal solution to the problems of living with my alcoholic, and now it was all accomplished in court in a matter of minutes. The tooth had been pulled, and I returned to work for the afternoon, telling no one of my new status. I had done what I set out to do, but there was no joy or sense of accomplishment. At best, it was the only solution I could find to the problems of alcoholism, not those that Sean faced but those that I did.

15

Learning the Truth
Summer 1969

The decree awarded me sole possession of the property, custody of the children, and a nominal amount of child support and alimony. There was never the slightest possibility that my husband could pay support, but it was important in that his non-payment would help build up a lien against the house and make it more difficult for him to sell.

As for custody of the children, there was no question—decree or no decree—but that they were mine and that I was singly responsible for their bed, board, clothing, health, education, morality and, the most sensitive area of all, their mental health and well-being. More than providing love and financial support, I wanted to give them confidence in themselves and a sense of security. I didn't want them to feel shame or guilt because their father was an alcoholic, a difficult task at best and more likely an impossible one because I never knew what was locked up inside. Yet I hoped that by keeping my alcoholic out of their lives with a separation I could make up for the past. Such was not the case.

Curtis, too sensitive to tune out at night, who couldn't help but hear the bad sounds, put his feelings in one of his poems, written when he was sixteen.

> O broken father
> who stole my pity
> who perpetuated my pain,
> my tearstained dreams
> are searching for you again.
> May your suffering be satisfied in me.
>
> In the pain of the night
> when tears are shed
> without reason
> and rest offers
> no answers,
> I sleep
> forcibly
> in the damp corners of alone
> touching uncertainty
> with thoughts of uncertain strength.
> Sweating
> in unconsciousness
> silence abounding
> through my own emptiness
> the night will be removed
> in tenderness,
> in time.

The damage had already been done, and there was more to come, decree or no decree. I had won my legal battle but not my war with alcoholism.

Convinced that my newly acquired legal document would guarantee a peaceful summer, I had rented the main house at substantially more rent than the cottage would bring and moved with the four boys into the cottage. The house tenants were wonderful family people with four children in a comparable age range, and there was much visiting back and forth and playing ball on the lawn.

As I was leaving the cottage to go to work one hot July morning, I saw a specter of the past: My alcoholic was playing ball with our youngest two sons and the youngest two of the tenants. I could see that Sean was very unsteady. His swollen stomach bulged over his faded blue bathing trunks, his legs were thin and bruised, and his gray hair was long, dirty and uncombed, with a yellowish tinge. I could also see the fixed, embarrassed smiles of Nicholas and Seamus.

I drove across the lawn in the Volkswagen and quietly told Sean he could not stay, as I now had legal possession of the house. He laughed and called out, "Go to hell!"

"Please leave," I repeated, "or I will have to call the police."

"Ha!" he shouted. "I don't care about you and your fucking police. Do you understand? This is my house and I'm here to stay, like it or not."

Like an autistic child who can't be reached by love or reason and no matter how tormented he was with guilt, I knew that my alcoholic was too far gone to care, to care what he was doing to himself or to his children, and I knew that if I gave an inch he'd be around for the summer. I drove straight to the police station, but by the time the officers came to the house Sean was gone. For the next ten days we played a game of hide-and-seek.

Driving home for lunch, I'd see his thin legs camouflaged by bushes, but by the time I could get to the phone he'd be gone. The boys said he sometimes came into the cottage at night, if I was out, telling them of his secret trips to Europe to spy on the "Russkies" and "Krauts," insisting that they turn off the lights and burn only a candle so that the agents out in the potato field couldn't find him. They told me these incidents in a kind of loving way, as if they were trying to protect their father, saying it was all right and I shouldn't get angry. Seamus justified one of his visits by saying, "Daddy came to the cottage smelling really bad, but then he took a nice bath and got all clean again." No matter how insane the scene, I was grateful that they could still care that much.

Once he came in while I was home for lunch. The children were out, and he said that if I tried to run or call the police he'd strangle me. So I sat and we began to chat. He told me he had just returned from Vietnam, killing, even though he hated the war and hated to have to kill, and that he had almost "gotten it" himself. And then he asked me if I had seen the film *Elvira Madigan*. I hadn't, and he said I should because it was very beautiful, beautifully photographed and a beautiful love story.

"Love is all that matters," he said gently. "You do still love me, don't you? That's all that really matters."

I said yes, because I did, and because in the most painful way that was all that really did matter. Then young Sean came in and I said I had to go back to work, knowing that our son, who was captain of both the football and wrestling teams at school, was big enough to contain his father. We smiled and said goodbye.

Loathing myself as usual, I went straight to the police, as Sean knew I would, because when they came he was gone again. There was a kind of Fellini madness, an almost fascinating but nightmarish quality, in the way he could make himself appear and disappear. And all the while the children were sharing the nightmare and, worse, sharing it with their friends. One day Nicholas called me at work to say, "Daddy's up at the beach again, and he's gone to the bathroom in his pants." How could I keep them from being ashamed?

During the week Sean was arrested for public intoxication. This was duly reported in the police-blotter column of the local newspaper along with the news that he had been placed in "the town lock-up." The drunk tank. The item was considered juicy enough to rate a little sub-headline in the blotter column and two paragraphs, and it made him sound like nothing more than the face on the barroom floor. Public intoxication was a crime or a joke but not symptomatic of a social problem or illness. I wondered if my locked-up drunk had read the item and if he would benefit from the redemptive powers of the press. It jumped out at me, and I ripped the offending page out of the paper in the hope that the children wouldn't see it; but naturally they found out about it and it made them ashamed. They wanted to believe their father was sick, but that was hard to do when he was publicly labeled a town drunk.

The next week the paper again reported his second arrest for public intoxication. Although I personally felt inured and considered the accounts just two more low blows at our unhappy plight —there was nothing I could do about the paper's editorial policy, and there was nothing I could do about my husband's alcoholism —I couldn't bear further humiliation for the children and went to the police. I said there was no point whatsoever in continuing to arrest him one day and then releasing him the next or as soon as he sobered up; he was sick and the next time it happened would they please call a doctor who could send my husband to the state hospital? The officer on duty gazed at me for several moments and then, turning to listen to the squawk box, mumbled he'd think about it. I called Eaton, who said to get Sean arrested for trespassing, and that way he'd get a longer sentence than for public intoxication.

A longer sentence. It takes time to learn to be subhuman, but I was learning, and if a "longer sentence" was the only way to keep my alcoholic out of town, then that's what it would have to be. The strain of trying to work (it was the height of the hectically busy summer season) and trying to protect the boys was more than I could bear. I went to the police and said that the next time I called I wanted my husband arrested for trespassing.

The next Sunday afternoon when I returned from the beach,

211

where I had gone to try to bleach my mind out in the sun, I found Sean passed out in the back of the VW, a pathetic-looking wreck, dirty, unshaven, sick. I went inside and called the police, staying in the kitchen to smoke and hide from the heartbreaking sight in the car. But when I heard the police I went out. I felt it was more honest. In his poor mixed-up mind, Sean had to know that it was I who was having him arrested so he wouldn't come back for more.

I then called the county medical officer and asked if he would commit my husband in lieu of his being sent to jail. He was a psychiatrist, and though I didn't know him, he sounded very intelligent and concerned. He said he would examine my husband and agreed that it was of no help to anyone to have him repeatedly locked up in jail.

I asked if he could suggest a long-range plan, and he answered in a voice that lacked conviction that possibly I could petition the courts to have my husband declared a nuisance and not be permitted in town, or, more likely, have his family present a united front, saying he either voluntarily commit himself to a hospital for a long period of time or they would cut off all resources if he didn't.

I told him I didn't have the money to keep hiring lawyers and that his family had, in the past, stood aside and would probably continue to do so.

In response he made the first direct and honest statement I had heard in five years: "I'm afraid the prospects for his recovery are dismal because, unfortunately, there is no set-up in our society —either legal or medical—for this kind of problem, even though it's a very common one."

During the week I learned that my alcoholic had been committed, and because he had an infected foot, caused when the police-car door was slammed on it, he was back in the medical wards. I called and asked to speak to the doctor in charge. This one had a slow, deep voice, with an accent that sounded Austrian, as did his name. He had attended Sean during his last commitment, and he told me that other than a badly infected foot, the patient seemed in fairly good condition.

"In good condition! How can he be?" I gasped. "Haven't you seen his swollen stomach, his distended navel, all the bruises?"

The doctor explained that the stomach condition was chronic with a damaged liver and that if the patient continued to drink he would slowly drink himself to death. I told him that I had first heard of his impending death two years ago, and since he was still alive, wasn't there any way to prevent this form of suicide?

"How long is the commitment for?" I asked.

"He was brought in on a fifteen-day health certificate," he answered.

"Then that's a waste of the taxpayers' money. All you can do in fifteen days is cure his foot so he can be released to go back out and drink himself to death," I said.

"H-m-m-m," he sighed, and then said that chronic alcoholism was very difficult to treat because treatment had to be voluntary, unless, of course, there was insanity, too. "You know," he continued in his slow, accented voice, "this is simply chronic alcoholism. There is no psychosis."

"No psychosis!" I almost shouted. "Then why is it that he can't work, that he hallucinates? Or simply why is it that he can't stop drinking?"

He answered that my husband had told him nothing about the hallucinations, and I interrupted to say that naturally my husband wouldn't talk about them when he was sober, as his main aim was to appear normal and sane so that he could be released to drink again. The doctor brushed this aside, saying that in any event these were all symptoms of chronic alcoholism and that the state hospital was for the severely disturbed, the real psychotics.

It was futile to try to change the direction of his thinking.

213

I must have sounded like just another rattled wife, trying to push a drunken bum out on the public charge; so I changed my tactics and asked him to please make the commitment for sixty days, as my husband was a devastating influence on the children and that he seriously impaired my ability to work and support them. A month later I received a notice from the hospital, saying that my husband had been discharged. This time Sean didn't come back to East Hampton.

∽16∽

May 12, 1970

One morning early in March I received a call from my sister-in-law. Although we had become estranged—except for the presents she sent the boys at Christmas, we had had no communication in over a year—I had always liked her. She was very intelligent and open, similar in many ways to Sean. After a rather guarded exchange of greetings, she said she had heard from her brother. He had called to say he had been hospitalized in New York for the past three months and now urgently wanted to straighten out his affairs. His lease on the apartment would be up soon, and he wasn't sure that he would renew it, so that he would need help in disposing of the furnishings. She said he sounded very weak, and immediately afterward she had called his doctor, a Dr. Pierce, who reported that the patient was in critical condition. She told me the name of the hospital and said she was going to visit Sean the next day and would call me back.

I had just begun my first paid vacation in five years of

working. Aside from having no money to go away, I was looking forward to two weeks of simply staying home and relaxing. The house I had rented for the winter was much nicer than the one we had lived in the previous year, well furnished, with a fireplace and two glass walls in the living room, with a view of the surrounding woods, and I was all set to sit and read, ride bikes with the boys, bake pies and cakes, to be only myself and a mother without the pressures of work or of dealing with lawyers, police, medical officers, and trying to contend with Sean.

All things considered, I felt we had made a fairly good adjustment. Young Sean was doing well at school. (Shortly after arriving there he wrote to me, "There is no doubt about it, there is much to learn and I plan to learn it. It will be rough but I am sure I can handle it." Like father like son. Or could this be a bad sign, an indication of incipient grandiosity?) Curtis, though still a poor scholar, was beginning to open up more and not spend so much time shut into his bedroom, and Seamus and Nicholas were much more carefree and doing well in school, with Seamus's reading now up to his grade level. They desperately wanted another dog, and I had secretly arranged to give them a Newfoundland puppy for Easter.

With the salary from my regular job, now raised to one hundred and fifty a week, and the extra money I earned on my party clinics and an occasional free-lance writing assignment from Marjorie, plus the continuing help from my father and two brothers-in-law, we were able to live comfortably. Curtis said that some of the kids at school actually thought we were rich. I had no outstanding debts of my own, and the monthly sheaf of bills and notices I received from State-Wide, World-Wide, Universal, and other all-consuming collection agencies I simply filed in the wastebasket. They were all for Sean's debts, and, being legally separated, I was no longer responsible for them; and had I been, there was no way I could have paid them.

Friends old and new had been wonderfully cordial to me,

and I had a pleasant enough social life, rarely entertaining but often entertained. Yet a day never went by that I didn't think about Sean, wondering what had happened to him. During the fall he had called a few times, always late at night and always sounding deranged, not conversing, just repeating over and over, "Where is love, where is love?" and I'd tell him that he should go to bed and then hang up. He stopped calling, and I had no news of him other than at Christmas when young Sean, home for vacation, said he had stopped by to see Dad when he was in New York.

"He was in terrible shape, Mom," he said, sounding very distressed, "and I wanted to stay with him, to show him that I loved him, but it was too sad, so I left. But the next day I felt guilty and I went back again. I really wanted to stay for a while, but I just couldn't, so I left."

I told him he had more guts that I did; at least he had tried to see his father, which was more than I could do. On New Year's Eve, a little tight and more than a little depressed, I had called the apartment, but there was no answer. Now, nearly three months later, I knew why. He had been in the hospital. He was dying. As soon as his sister hung up I dialed Information for the hospital number, but I didn't call. After all I had done to him, the strait jacket, institutions, jails, running away, what could I possibly say to him? I didn't have the courage to call until evening, after a martini, a bracer. Then I went into the bedroom and shut the door so the children wouldn't hear me. I felt I was calling a long-estranged lover, one who had to care enough to understand and forgive me.

He said hello in a soft, tired voice. "Sean," I blurted out through tears I couldn't stop. "It's me."

There was a long pause, and then I heard his quiet, lovely laugh. "It's really you. Oh, darling, my darling, I'm laughing and crying. I can't believe it's really you."

As I was riding to the hospital the next day the cab driver

told me he reckoned this was the only hospital in the city he hadn't been in. "Kep' bustin' my head open gettin' drunk," he said, laughing, "and no one could tell me nothin'. Then one day I got smart."

"Did you join AA?" I asked. How had we ever hit on this topic?

"Me!" he chortled. "No, ma'm, not me. I just got smart, got tired of gettin' my head busted in." And my beautiful, brainy husband was dying now because he had never gotten that smart.

Sean was slumped to one side of the pillows, a broken, discarded boy doll. His eyes were closed and his face was very pale and thin and his hair was snow white, and yet he looked young, very much as when we first met. The hospital gown had slipped off one shoulder, a shoulder too strong and broad for the thin arms that rested by his side, one receiving blood, the other with a rosary wrapped around it, like a baby's identification bracelet. The sheet was stretched over the round ball of his stomach.

I had never really believed that alcohol would kill him. Now I had to believe it. My husband was dying and the past was unredeemable and there was no way to make up for those awful years. I sat by his bed, trying to stifle the sound of my tears, but he opened his eyes and after a moment smiled that lovely crooked grin that showed very even white teeth.

"Oh, darling," I sobbed, "how could we have been such fools?"

"I wish we could go back to the way it was," he said, reaching out one arm to me, and we held each other and laughed and cried.

Later that afternoon I stood outside his room and talked to Dr. Pierce. It had been five years since he had told me, over the phone, that there was nothing he could do for Sean; now, however, he sounded very positive. He told me in his cool, firm voice that everything possible was being done for my husband but that the disease was taking its "inexorable course." Now he had a patient with a real disease—cirrhosis of the liver—and the master medic was at the helm.

Jaws set, I gazed past him as he calmly reeled off his little collection of medical data: thirty pounds of fluid passed, staph infection cleared, intravenous feedings, special diet to keep body fluids balanced, daily blood transfusions, something about the scar tissue on my husband's heart, all a neat, clinical and meaningless accounting of a hopeless situation.

As I listened I kept thinking, "What in the hell good is your splendid treatment doing now that Sean is dying? He needed help five years ago, when it wasn't too late, before he became so completely and helplessly addicted." But I was too close to tears to speak, and also I knew in my heart that Sean's dying wasn't his doctor's fault. Until research comes through with the magic bullet to stop the progression of the disease, or until there is a way to enforce abstinence and provide prolonged psychiatric treatment, there was really nothing this particular doctor could have done for Sean. He had probably never even been trained in the treatment of alcoholism.

Then Dr. Pierce, tipping his hat to what fools we other mortals are, said that during the past three months my husband had, of course, been kicking himself around the block for all the drinking. Professional cool was one thing, playing the Dutch uncle another.

"But he couldn't help it," I protested, my eyes filling with tears. "He couldn't help himself. He was too sick. There was no way in this whole rotten system to help him. I tried, but I couldn't."

"No, you couldn't," he said matter-of-factly, "but you couldn't live with this kind of a problem either, could you?" he intoned. I suppose he was trying to comfort me.

I took a deep breath and after a minute said, "He looks as if he's starving to death."

"That's precisely what's happening," he answered, explaining that the patient had practically no liver left and couldn't digest food.

"How will he die?"

"Either metabolically or hemorrhaging. If the stomach becomes too distended, the blood vessels in the lining in effect explode and the lungs fill with blood," he answered.

"How long can he live?"

"It could be two days, or two weeks, not much longer. But," he added on the upswing, "he has an iron constitution. I'm surprised he's lasted this long." How I loathed that doctor.

But he didn't die in two days or two weeks. His iron constitution and the fact that he didn't want to die kept him going. He was able to eat more and take the medicine that had made him gag before, and his stomach became less distended. I brought him a shamrock plant and pictures of the children and the new Newfoundland puppy and told him about our house in the woods. Now that he was sober we could talk, once again, about the future, even though it didn't exist, and he asked, almost shyly, if there would be room for him at home and if he could come and help take care of things and train the dog until he was well enough to work again.

We could also talk about the past and now without recriminations or without skirting the central fact of his alcoholism. It pleased me—and meant more to me than anything anyone else had said—when he told me he was proud of me for managing to make a go of it with nothing; and I told him that I had never blamed him, that whatever had happened had happened because he was a victim of alcoholism.

But he said no.

"It wasn't the alcohol—that was just a symptom. I had too much responsibility when I was too young, too much responsibility without the authority to carry it off. And then, when I got older, after the war and law school, I wanted to be a big shot, and I lost track of what really mattered, you and the boys and our life together. I got off the track and I couldn't get back. We had everything, didn't we, and I threw it all away. I lost everything, even my reputation," he said wistfully.

Listening, I wondered if, after only three months in the hospital, the longest period of sobriety he had known in the past seven years except when he was incarcerated with the "real nuts" for ninety days, he had come to recognize his "grandiosity," the term used by the psychiatrist who had treated him the first time he was hospitalized. And I wondered how that doctor, after only four or five sessions, a mere beginning in psychotherapy, could have written Sean off as a hopeless alcoholic, saying, "He has, for want of a better word, grandiosity, and I doubt if he ever gets over it." An alcoholic he certainly was, a man who had been continually drunk for a year; but he was also a loving man whose wife had run off with his children, a proud man who had been thrown in Bellevue, "with niggers kneeling on my chest," and a sick man who had suffered a liver failure. Perhaps if he had been merely insane, instead of damned by an addiction to alcohol, the doctor might have treated him as a man too weak, spiritually and physically, to admit, explain or understand what had gone wrong with his life, a man gradually overwhelmed by a deep depression, a cumulative despair that began when his father died and festered and grew, a depression he tried to obliterate with drink, more and more until drink was all that mattered to him. I remembered how in my dejection that last winter we lived together in East Hampton I too had turned to the bottle, not, to my knowledge, because of a sense of grandiosity but because liquor was the most immediate means of escape.

Again and again I asked myself what I could have done differently. Why couldn't I have loved him the right way, enough to save him? When I was away from him I knew he was going to die, but when I was with him I couldn't believe it. The nurses kept telling me he was their favorite patient, "so handsome and so intelligent," and the man who shared his room (his wife was always bringing him special foods from home and taking home the special hospital food he wouldn't eat) grumbled that it made no sense for a handsome young man like my husband to be so sick, a man "who talked so good," a man with an education. "Doctor doesn't care what happens to him," he grumbled, "just comes in here, picks up his arm and then throws it down, like he was dirt."

But even before he said that I had become obsessed with the wild idea that, liver or no, he had to live, that he could be saved by a doctor who cared. I called my doctor friend, Jim, and asked him to check on the treatment Sean was getting (Dr. Pierce icily mentioned the call), and Jim assured me that everything was being done, including calling in a liver specialist for consultation. But that wasn't enough for me, and I called Marjorie, and she put me in touch with one of the heads of the National Council on Alcoholism, a doctor. He offered to call in another liver specialist, saying, however, that he was afraid it was too late.

One day, early in May, Sean answered my inevitable "How are you feeling?" by saying very calmly, "I've been here for four months and I don't seem to be getting any better. And I don't want to spend the rest of my life lying around in hospitals." From then on he slept most of the time, absolutely immobile except when a frown of pain would cross his forehead. I sat on the foot of his bed and smoked and tried to read from the collection of books he had by his bed or just cried quietly. Other times I sat beside him, my arm around him and his head on my shoulder, the reverse of the way it was on those mornings long ago when we had our moments together before the children got up. He nodded when I spoke to him and dutifully, like a child, ate when I fed him and tried to return my kisses as best he could. Once I asked him if he wanted a puff of my cigarette and he smiled and nodded; it was something to share. If I had had a drink, I'm afraid I would have offered him that, too.

I didn't know what to do about bringing the children to see him. Even though I saw him again as the man he really was, it didn't follow that the children would. He was their father, but he was also a dying man, emaciated and estranged, separated from them by too many bad scenes and, more, by his own torment and suffering. He was in pain much of the time and didn't press to see the boys except to say that he wanted to talk to the oldest, Sean. I called him at his prep school and told him to come to New York. At first he sounded reluctant, saying he had already had too many heart-to-heart talks with Dad when he was drunk; but of course he did come, bringing with him his old pal Phil, the one who had so politely said of the passed-out figure on the floor, "Gosh, your father sure is tired." I wasn't there, but I'm sure young Sean did everything right and that Phil provided the needed emotional support.

I decided not to take Seamus to the hospital. He was now eleven and since the age of four had known his father only as an alcoholic. Not knowing whether I was doing right or wrong, I decided it would be better if he could resurrect a memory from snapshots of happier times, rather than once again seeing his father in another devastating situation. I told Nicholas and Curtis that they should go to the hospital. Nicholas immediately agreed, but when he came with me he could only sit in shocked silence for half an hour. It was just as we were leaving that he managed to tell his father that he was on the high honor roll, played football on the first team, and was class president. Sean smiled and nodded, but he was by then too weak for praise and comment. Curtis kept saying he would go (the boys came into the city over their Easter vacation), but he never did, and I didn't want to make an issue of his visit. Maybe he thought it was more than he could bear.

Except for a single visit from his sister and brother Dan, I don't think anyone else came to see Sean. Dan said he simply didn't have the courage to come back, and I think that was the reason our close friends stayed away. It couldn't have been the fact alone that he was dying, nor, I'm sure, the supposition that he was dying of some dirty disease, an insatiable, destructive craving for alcohol. I think, rather, that his dying seemed so unnecessary and so futile, and deep down those who knew him well felt they couldn't face this senseless failure and waste of life.

I couldn't be with him all the time because I had no one to stay with the children in East Hampton, and though they could manage for a night or two I didn't like to leave them alone any longer. So I went back and forth twice a week. The weekend of May 9 and 10 was unseasonably hot, in the nineties, and as I sat on Sean's bed that Saturday I remembered how much he used to sweat and how our bodies slid against each other on stifling New York nights before we could afford an air conditioner. Now his skin was very cool and dry.

The floor nurse kept telling me that I should go home and get some rest, and around four I left. I was staying with an old Bennington chum (we had introduced her to her future husband, a friend of Sean's, at the business school when my lover was at Harvard studying law; they were long since divorced), the best person I could have stayed with because Suzanne really liked Sean, one of my few friends who could take him, however. Once she'd said he was more interesting drunk than 99 percent of the rest of the world sober. But I was too depleted to see even her and went instead to Bloomingdale's, a place to get lost in the crowd and cool off in the air-conditioning. And I knew I would need a pair of black shoes for the funeral.

The ones I liked best, simple and well made, were fifty dollars.

"They're awfully expensive," I said to the clerk.

"Fiorentina," he shrugged, "the Cadillac of shoes."

I had a black dress, three years old, but it would do with the right shoes. I remembered Sean's note: "I know, too, that my luck will run out, so hang in there and all your problems will be solved." With the insurance, my financial worries would be over, and I wanted to look right at his funeral, not tacky, but like his wife, the way he liked me to look. He always said I had the most beautiful legs in the world. I bought the shoes.

I went back to the hospital on Sunday morning and late in

the afternoon kissed him and whispered goodbye. He nodded ever so slightly, his eyes still closed. At the door I said goodbye again, and he opened his eyes and tried to smile, just a flicker of his crooked grin. On Tuesday morning Dr. Pierce called me in East Hampton to tell me my husband was dead. It was May 12, our nineteenth wedding anniversary.

Although no one had come to see Sean in the hospital, many came to his funeral—doctors, lawyers, judges, an architect, several journalists, an artist—all who had admired and liked my husband and, I'm sure, would have helped him had they known how. I was glad, especially for the children. I wanted them to know their father had been a fine man, with many fine friends, and they commented later on the large turnout. Several of their former New York school friends came, too, and that also pleased them and me. And though I know it is a meaningless statement, I know it would have pleased Sean. He loved kids.

The boys said they'd like to have some of their kind of music played at the funeral because they knew how much Dad had liked Bob Dylan and how they used to perform for him when they were all little, gyrating and cavorting about, banging on the bottoms of wastebaskets and holding a broom for a microphone, pretending to be a group Sean called The Grasshoppers. They asked for a new Beatles song, "Let It Be." It sounded just right on the church organ, tender and loving and very much in harmony with the simplicity of the Mass. My husband's agony was over, and even though he was lying dead in the white-draped coffin at the altar, we were together again as a family, in love and dignity, in the compassion of God. I didn't want the Mass to end.

At the wake the preceding night the priest, whom I did not know, told me about the funeral Mass and mentioned that he would deliver the homily. I had taken a tranquilizer and nodded.

But the next day, just as we were going into the church, I asked the priest what he was going to say in the homily. He said he was going to speak of this day not as one mourning the death of my husband but as a celebration of his rebirth into a new life in heaven.

"Then, please," I said, "no homily."

I don't know how much I believe in the solace of the hereafter, in a heaven, but I did know I did not believe my husband's death was a cause for celebration. The odds against him had been too brutal. He died at the age of forty-five because, although alcoholism is said to be a disease, it isn't treated as such—not medically nor legally nor socially—and I can't "Let It Be."